United States Higher Education and World Affairs

INDIANA UNIVERSITY COMMITTEE ON INTERNATIONAL AFFAIRS, 1963-66*

HERMAN B WELLS (Chairman), Chancellor of the University; President, Indiana University Foundation

HOWARD T. BATCHELDER, Director of Graduate Studies, School of Education; Associate Dean, School of Education

EDWARD H. BUEHRIG, Professor of Government

CECIL K. BYRD, Associate Director of Libraries, University Librarian (1965-66)

ROBERT F. BYRNES, Professor of History; Director, International Affairs Center

ARTHUR S. DANIELS, Dean of the School of Health, Physical Education, and Recreation (Deceased, June, 1966) (1965-66)

NICHOLAS DEWITT, Associate Professor of Economics and Government (1963-64 and 1965-66)

LAURIE M. GUNTER, Professor of Nursing (1965-66)

RAY L. HEFFNER, JR., Vice-President and Dean of the Faculties (1965-66)

PAUL KLINGE, Executive Associate in the Indiana University Foundation (1964-65)

LAWRENCE C. LARSON, Associate Dean of the Division of University Extension; Director, Audio-Visual Center

WALTER H. C. LAVES, Chairman, Department of Government

J. GUS LIEBENOW, Chairman, African Studies Program; Professor of Government (1965-66)

DORIS H. MERRITT, Assistant Dean for Medical Research, Assistant Professor of Pediatrics

LYNNE L. MERRITT, JR., Vice-President for Research and Dean of Advanced Studies (1964-65 and 1965-66)

DAVID MITCHELL, Chairman and Professor of Oral Diagnosis, School of Medicine (1965-66)

ROBERT E. QUIRK, Professor of History (1963-64 and 1964-65)

T. EDWIN RANDALL, Assistant Treasurer

FRED W. RIGGS, Professor of Government

STEFAN H. ROBOCK, Director and Professor of International Business Administration, School of Business

JAMES R. SCOBIE, Chairman of the Committee on Latin American Studies; Professor of History (1965-66)

JOSEPH L. SUTTON, Dean of the College of Arts and Sciences (1964-65 and 1965-66)

WIENCZYSLAW J. WAGNER, Professor of Law (1965-66)

EDGAR L. WILLIAMS, Chairman and Professor of Personnel and Organization Behavior, School of Business (1965-66)

RICHARD F. CRABBS (Executive Secretary), Special Assistant for International Affairs, International Affairs Center

*Titles current in June, 1966

 PRAEGER SPECIAL STUDIES IN
INTERNATIONAL POLITICS AND PUBLIC AFFAIRS

United States Higher Education and World Affairs

A PARTIALLY ANNOTATED BIBLIOGRAPHY

**Richard F. Crabbs
Frank W. Holmquist**

Published in cooperation with the
Indiana University Committee on International Affairs

FREDERICK A. PRAEGER, Publishers
New York · Washington · London

The purpose of the Praeger Special Studies is to make specialized research monographs in U.S. and international economics and politics available to the academic, business, and government communities. For further information, write to the Special Projects Division, Frederick A. Praeger, Publishers, 111 Fourth Avenue, New York, N.Y. 10003.

FREDERICK A. PRAEGER, PUBLISHERS
111 Fourth Avenue, New York, N.Y. 10003, U.S.A.
77-79 Charlotte Street, London W.1, England

Published in the United States of America in 1967
by Frederick A. Praeger, Inc., Publishers

All rights reserved

© 1967 by Frederick A. Praeger, Inc.

Library of Congress Catalog Card Number: 66-21775

Printed in the United States of America

FOREWORD

The responsibilities of American universities and colleges in world affairs include many dimensions--teaching, conducting research, exchange of persons, and cooperation with educational institutions and efforts abroad. To match the kind of world in which we live, American universities' present programs of teaching, research, and service must be broadened and deepened. Anything less is inadequate to meet their obligations to their students, to the American government, and to the world of learning.

The content of courses, as every factual study shows, is tragically parochial. Most of them are entirely Western-oriented, and this at a time when the United States is involved in the affairs of nations, both new and old, in every corner of the globe. We surely need to understand the points of view of other nations if our relations with them are to be fruitful.

In the field of research, something has been accomplished in the last twenty years, largely thanks to the help of our great foundations, Ford, Rockefeller, Carnegie, and the others; but I think that those who have been in the thick of that work would agree that we have barely scratched the surface. A massive effort in research will not only give us the knowledge we need to revise our curriculum content and to carry on our foreign relations, but it will also help us to develop a reservoir of expertise which we especially need if we are to fill our role in the world.

Public service is deeply ingrained in the state universities and land-grant colleges and also in the other institutions of higher education. They owe a debt of public service to the community, the state, the nation, and now, I would say, to the world of rising expectations. After all, most of our educational institutions were developed in the last century and were directly related to the problem of assisting a pioneer society to develop rapidly. It is therefore not strange that the newer nations of the world find it desirable to have our type of education available to them--a situation which places an extra measure of responsibility on us.

This bibliography spans the field of the different types of involvement of United States higher education with world affairs. It is a useful and unique tool for those concerned with the problems and opportunities that this field presents. As such, it offers a contribution and public service in the best traditions of American education.

                                      Herman B Wells
                                      Chancellor, Indiana University

PREFACE

This bibliography began in 1964 as a service to the members of the Indiana University Committee on International Affairs. The committee, at the request of President Elvis J. Stahr, was reviewing the university's international teaching, research, and service programs both at home and abroad, in content as well as in organizational terms. One result of the committee's work has been the establishment of the International Affairs Center, headed by Professor Robert F. Byrnes. The center performs a service and coordinating role under the direction of the Vice President for Research and Dean of Advanced Studies, Lynne L. Merritt, Jr. The committee, under the chairmanship of Chancellor Herman B Wells, continues its broad review and advisory role.

Meanwhile, the bibliographic effort revealed a rich lode of study, thought, and recommendation about the various aspects of college and university international commitments. Although the list is not exhaustive, it is fairly extensive and includes a number of items not easily identifiable otherwise. The committee has therefore consented to making the bibliography available to others concerned with the international role of colleges and universities. Entries of particular interest to students of the international field are marked with an asterisk.

The debts we have accumulated during this enterprise have been many and heavy; to both individuals and institutions we express admiration and appreciation. All who have participated in international education in some way are involved; some have distilled experience for the benefit of colleagues; a few have provided bibliographies which have contributed immeasurably to the present product. We are particularly grateful to staff members of Education and World Affairs and the Institute of International Education and to our colleagues on the faculty of Indiana University, especially Professor Walter H. C. Laves.

Happy, willing, and incredibly devoted assistance from a bevy of charming ladies has made the bibliography possible. An intellectual and emotional partner in the enterprise was Mrs. Richard Myren, who applied a librarian's eye to citations and preparing the index. Mrs. John Strikis provided skill and artistry in the typing. Mrs. Robert Tennyson aided greatly with the editing. Mrs. Chris Wagner and Mrs. Samuel Boyd assisted the enterprise in a variety of ways.

Bloomington, Indiana

Richard F. Crabbs
Frank W. Holmquist

CONTENTS

	Page
FOREWORD	v
PREFACE	vii

PART I. INTERNATIONAL EDUCATIONAL ACTIVITY

Chapter
1. PHILOSOPHY, ORGANIZATION, AND GENERAL DISCUSSION ... 3

PART II. CURRICULA

2. THE INTERNATIONAL CONTENT OF UNDERGRADUATE CURRICULA ... 17
3. THE INTERNATIONAL CONTENT OF TEACHER EDUCATION CURRICULA ... 23
4. AREA STUDIES ... 25

    Philosophy and General Discussion ... 25
    Africa ... 33
    Asia ... 34
    Latin America ... 40
    Middle East ... 41
    Russia and Eastern Europe ... 41

5. TRAINING FOR INTERNATIONAL SERVICE ... 43

    General ... 43
    Peace Corps ... 50

PART III. EDUCATIONAL EXCHANGE

6. GENERAL DISCUSSION OF EDUCATIONAL EXCHANGE ... 55
7. HISTORY OF EDUCATIONAL EXCHANGE ... 60
8. RESEARCH ON EDUCATIONAL EXCHANGE ... 63

PART IV. EDUCATIONAL EXCHANGE: UNITED STATES NATIONALS ABROAD

9   UNITED STATES STUDENTS ABROAD   69

      Philosophy, Curricula, and Organization   69
      Attitudes and Adjustment   74

10   UNITED STATES TEACHERS AND SCHOLARS ABROAD   76

PART V. EDUCATIONAL EXCHANGE: FOREIGN NATIONALS IN THE UNITED STATES

11   FOREIGN STUDENTS   81

      Philosophy, Curricula, and Organization   81
      Attitudes and Adjustment   96
      Admission and Credential Evaluation   109

12   TRAINING FOREIGN SPECIALISTS IN THE UNITED STATES   114

13   ALUMNI, RETURNEES, AND PROGRAM EVALUATIONS   117

PART VI. INSTITUTIONAL RELATIONSHIPS IN INTERNATIONAL EDUCATION

14   UNITED STATES GOVERNMENT POLICY   131

15   HIGHER EDUCATION AND THE UNITED STATES GOVERNMENT   146

16   HIGHER EDUCATION AND INTERNATIONAL ORGANIZATIONS   151

17   HIGHER EDUCATION AND INTERNATIONAL DEVELOPMENT   153

PART VII. RESOURCE MATERIALS

18   HANDBOOKS, GUIDES, AND REFERENCE WORKS   171

19   BIBLIOGRAPHIES   178

CONTENTS xi

APPENDIX A: ORGANIZATIONS WITH MAJOR INTERESTS
  IN HIGHER EDUCATION AND WORLD AFFAIRS   185

AUTHOR INDEX   197

ABOUT THE AUTHORS   209

PART I

INTERNATIONAL EDUCATIONAL ACTIVITY

CHAPTER 1 PHILOSOPHY, ORGANIZATION, AND GENERAL DISCUSSION

*1. Allen, Herman R. <u>Open Door to Learning; The Land-Grant System Enters Its Second Century</u>. Urbana: University of Illinois Press, 1963. Pp. 193.

The volume contains study-group reports presented at the Land-Grant Centennial Convocation at Kansas City, Missouri, November 12-16, 1961. Various aspects of international education are discussed: (a) international affairs; (b) the foreign student, scholar, and trainee in the United States; (c) education of Americans for service overseas; and (d) recommendations on international affairs. The recommendations assume added significance because they reflect the "official" thinking of representatives of many of America's most important institutions of higher learning.

2. Bolling, Landrum R. "A Small College Discovers the World," <u>Overseas</u>, III (April, 1964), 12-17.

<u>Overseas</u> was formerly titled <u>Institute of International Education: News Bulletin</u>.

3. Bowles, Frank H. "American Responsibilities in International Education," <u>Educational Record</u>, XLV (Winter, 1964), 19-26.

In its deep involvement in international education, the United States has scattered its commitments between those benefiting students and those aiding governments. Several generalizations are drawn from an examination of these commitments. (a) Concentration has shifted away from student support to government support.

(b) The purposes of supporting foreign educational systems have not been stated explicitly. (c) A lack of knowledge of foreign educational systems and insufficient manpower handicap the United States in keeping commitments. (d) Secondary school experts are not sufficiently utilized. (e) The American commitment to international education is understaffed at the policy level. (f) In the future the emphasis must shift from political and economic ends to a full exchange of ideas.

4. The College and University in International Affairs. New York: Carnegie Foundation for the Advancement of Teaching, 1960. Pp. 15.

    The broad range of topics includes undergraduate and graduate curricula in international affairs, foreign student education on American campuses, international scholarly communication, university-government overseas contracts, and general international responsibilities of universities in world affairs.

5. Drucker, Peter F. "American Higher Education: Cornerstone of Free World Unity," Platform for Higher Education; Guidelines for the Sixties: Current Issues in Higher Education, 1960. Ed. G. Kerry Smith. Proceedings, 15th Annual National Conference on Higher Education, Association for Higher Education, Chicago, March 6-9, 1960, pp. 17-23.

    Drucker opens by stating that "the American college and university has become the most effective international force today. . . ." He points out that educators in the United States have done a better job than is generally known, and they have done it in a quiet manner. Yet educators do not fully realize their gigantic power and responsibility in the teaching of foreign students.

*6. Education and World Affairs. The University Looks Abroad: Approaches to World Affairs at Six Universities. New York: Walker & Co., 1965. Pp. 300.

    The six American universities included in this survey are Stanford, Michigan State, Tulane,

Wisconsin, Cornell, and Indiana. In an introduction, William W. Marvel, president of Education and World Affairs, reviews the evolution of the international dimension in university education and states that rather "than embark at this time on a long and elaborate national survey, it seemed relevant from the standpoint of present needs to sight in on the specific lines of development on particular campuses--to seek the big picture of 'where we are' in 1965 by bringing certain leading universities successively before the camera lens." A helpful summary chapter concludes. The bibliography includes extracts from this bibliography.

7. Frankel, Charles. "New Initiatives in International Education," from an address delivered at the 1965 meeting of the National Association of State Universities and Land-Grant Colleges, Journal of Higher Education, XXXVII (March, 1966), 121-28.

8. Gange, John. University Research on International Affairs. Washington, D.C.: American Council on Education, 1958. Pp. 147.

    The author is concerned with (a) the relation of research to the understanding of world affairs, (b) the administrative setting of research in academic institutions, (c) the relative merits of individual and group research, and (d) the problem of access to materials. A bibliography is included.

9. Harrington, Fred Harvey. "University Involvement in International Affairs," Higher Education in the United States. Report of the 9th Annual Midwest Conference of Fulbright Scholars, June 10-14, 1962. Madison: University of Wisconsin, 1962, pp. 14-24.

*10. Henry, David D. "The American University Looks Abroad: View from the President's Office," a paper delivered at the regional conference of Education and World Affairs, East Lansing, Michigan, October 11, 1963. Mimeo. Pp. 12.

    Noting that "a coherent, sharply defined rationale for the role of international service in the American university" has not yet been developed, the author raises significant questions and provides some answers to the problem of effectively utilizing foreign students, faculty with overseas experience, the curriculum, and consortia activities in pursuit of a desirable international role for the university. Meanwhile, dual commitments to the constituency which supports the university and to the community of learning in general must be recognized.

11. Houle, Cyril O., and Nelson, Charles A. *The University, The Citizen, and World Affairs*. Prepared for the Carnegie Endowment for International Peace and others. Washington, D.C.: American Council on Education, 1956. Pp. 179.

    The central question of this publication is how to educate adults in world affairs. Universities play a central role in this process and should have the following objectives in common: (a) to help make inattentive citizens attentive, (b) to serve the continuing needs of attentive citizens for background information and understanding, (c) to encourage some attentive citizens to become active, (d) to serve the continuing needs of active citizens for a basic understanding of world affairs, (e) to help the active citizens find the means to meet their responsibilities, and (f) to provide the opportunity for specialists to educate one another. A thorough discussion of how universities might attain these objectives is presented.

12. Hughes, Emmet John (ed.). *Education in World Perspective*. International Conference on World Educational Problems, Poughkeepsie, N.Y., 1961. New York: Harper & Row, 1962. Pp. 201.

    Papers from a conference, March 19-24, 1961, at Vassar College on "Emerging Values and New Directions, Their Implications for Education." The breadth of the conference theme gives an indication of the diversity of approaches: economic and social development, political interaction, and the relation of the individual to society. The messages of this truly international group of women emphasize the urgency of an international outlook in today's revolutionary world.

13. Humphrey, Richard A. *Education Without Boundaries*. Addresses and proceedings from the

4th Annual Conference on University Contracts Abroad, Washington, November 13-14, 1958. Washington, D.C.: American Council on Education, 1959. Pp. 68.

Addresses include "The Educational Challenge in Underdeveloped Countries," Leonard J. Saccio; "Observations on Foreign Relations of American Universities," Dean Rusk; "Cultural Problems in Overseas Education and Operation," Norman Burns; and "Effectiveness of U.S. Educational Efforts for Non-Americans Here and Abroad," Robert Rupard.

14. Hunnicutt, Clarence W. (ed.). *America's Emerging Role in Overseas Education*. Syracuse, N.Y.: Syracuse University Press, 1962.

15. *Improving International Understanding Through Binational Education*. Atlanta, Ga.: Southern Association of Colleges and Schools, 1962.

16. "Inter-American Issue," *Institute of International Education: News Bulletin*, XXXIV (October, 1958), entire issue.

17. "International Education: Two Essays." ("Occasional Paper," No. 65-103.) Mimeo., Center for the Study of Educational Policy, Department of History and Philosophy of Education, School of Education, Indiana University, 1965. Pp. 31.

The two essays are "A Teaching College for the World," R. Freeman Butts, and "Education and Intercultural Understanding," Stanley E. Ballinger. Butts asserts that education is the single greatest force for modernization and development. It is essential that the aid-giving West recognize the value of education and foster it without regard to traditional concepts of tutelage as in past aid-giving programs. The university is designated as the ideal institution to promote this "selfless" idea of education. Ballinger believes intercultural education demands the prerequisite of understanding ourselves and our way of doing things. Our schools must seek better ways to teach the ability to help others with empathy but without imposition.

18. "International Educational Activities of American Universities and Colleges," a report of the Commission on Education and International Affairs of the American Council on Education, April 17, 1957, <u>Educational Record</u>, XXXVIII (October, 1957), 382-408.

    A survey of 852 institutions reveals the views of American educators on international education policies and provides data on the extent of American university participation in international education. Focusing on university--Federal government relationships, the report finds a consensus that American higher education should (a) work toward the general agreement that the broad purpose of international educational activities is to educate for greater intercultural understanding, (b) insist on a greater voice in decisions regarding government-financed activities of the university overseas, and (c) insure better channels of communication between the university and various government agencies.

19. Kelsey, Clyde E., Jr. "A New Dimension of Responsibility for Higher Education," <u>Educational Record</u>, XLVI (Fall, 1965), 346-50.

20. Laves, Walter H. C. "The Role of Institutions of Higher Learning in Developing Asian-United States Relations," <u>Educational Record</u>, XXXIX (July, 1958), 287-92.

    Noting the necessity for mutual understanding between the peoples of Asia and America, Professor Laves urges that universities play a central role in meeting this goal. Three research proposals are suggested--factors contributing to mutual tension, information media and content shaping our attitudes toward each other, and curricular improvement at all levels. More effort should be put into general curricular revision, educational exchange programs, and governmental cooperation with UNESCO.

21. McGrath, Earl J. "American Educators and International Affairs," <u>Teachers College Record</u>, LXI (October, 1959), 10-22.

22. McKeon, Richard. "Universities in the Modern World" in <u>Issues in University Education</u>.

Ed. Charles Frankel. New York: Harper & Row, 1959, pp. 1-23.

23. Malik, Charles H. "Reflections on the International School," Educational Record, XLIV (July, 1963), 282-87.

24. Marvel, William W. "American Higher Education in Service Abroad," Liberal Education, XLIX (December, 1963), 541-52.

25. _____. "A Dilemma for our Colleges and Universities: Domestic Demands and Overseas Needs," Critical Decisions in Higher Education: Current Issues in Higher Education, 1963. Ed. G. Kerry Smith. Proceedings, 18th Annual National Conference on Higher Education, Association for Higher Education, Chicago, March 3-6, 1963, pp. 128-31.

26. Nason, John W. "Colleges Must Reassess Their International Resources," Overseas, III (April, (1964), 4-6.

27. Neal, Joe W. "Developing the International Office," Overseas, III (April, 1964), 7-11.

Elaborating on his experience at the University of Texas, the author urges that universities create a strong and highly centralized international office with supervision from only the top administrators.

> Only by bringing all international program activities under the international office can they be related to each other and clearly identified with the over-all international role of the institution. Thus it is necessary to remove the programs from the agencies to which they were initially assigned.

Foreign student programming, special overseas projects, education abroad, and community programs should be the core operations of the international office.

28. Parthemos, George S. (ed.). Higher Education in a World of Conflict. Athens: University of Georgia Press, 1962. Pp. 186.

29. Phillips, Claude S., Jr. "The Present World Challenge to Higher Education," <u>Educational Record</u>, XLIV (July, 1963), 266-74.

   The author pleads for a redefinition of the educated man. "We must ask whether the horizon of our concept of a university has widened so as to embrace a truly world-wide concept of truth and a truly world-wide spectrum of social needs." Even with advances made, the colleges and universities have not fully grasped the significance of a rapidly changing world and a corresponding increase of United States involvement in it.

30. Phillips, Ethel C. <u>The Record and the Vision</u>. A Report on American Voluntary Associations and International Cooperation. New York: Published for the United Nations Association of the United States of America by Interchange, 1966. Pp. 80.

*31. <u>Report of the Committee on Culture and Intellectual Exchange of the National Citizens' Commission on International Cooperation to The White House Conference on International Cooperation</u>, November 28-December 1, 1965. Washington, D.C.: Government Printing Office, 1965.

   Report by a number of distinguished private citizens with several explicit recommendations for both private and governmental initiative on international aspects of such topics as publishing and writing, library exchange, world languages, ethnic relations, student exchange, international travel, architecture, painting, sculpture, crafts, music, theater and dance, motion pictures, radio and television, newspapers and periodicals, business corporations, and technological change.

32. <u>The Responsibility of Higher Education for Helping to Develop International Understanding</u>. A series of papers presented at the Annual Meeting of the American Council on Education, October 6, 1955. Washington, D.C.: American Council on Education, 1956. Pp. 22. (Reprinted from <u>Educational Record</u>, April, 1956.)

   Topics and authors include "What Institutions of Higher Education Are Doing in Their Teaching

PHILOSOPHY, ORGANIZATION, AND GENERAL DISCUSSION 11

and Activity Programs," Howard E. Wilson; "Student Exchanges," Donald J. Shank; "Other Exchange Programs at the Higher Education Level," John Holden; "Cultural Exchanges Involving Institutions of Higher Learning," Dan M. Lacy; "Discussion of the Papers," Helen Bragdon.

33. Scanlon, David G. (ed.). *International Education: A Documentary History.* New York: Bureau of Publications, Teachers' College, Columbia University, 1960. Pp. 196.

    A volume particularly valuable to someone trying to understand how the concept of international education has evolved. The editor's introductory essay provides an orientation to the primary sources.

34. Stevenson, William E. "American Higher Education and World Involvement," *Educational Record*, XLII (January, 1961), 21-27.

35. Taggart, Glen L. "International Program Developments at Michigan State University," *Institute of International Education: News Bulletin*, XXXIII (January, 1958), 9-12.

36. Taylor, Harold. "The Idea of a World College," *Phi Delta Kappan*, XLIV (June, 1963), 399-402.

37. Tewksbury, Donald G. "American Education and the International Scene," *Teachers College Record*, LX (April, 1959), 357-68.

*38. *The University and World Affairs.* Report of the Committee on the University and World Affairs. New York: The Ford Foundation, 1960. Pp. 84. Available from Education and World Affairs.

    Since publication, the report, which was solicited by the United States Department of State, has exerted strong influence on subsequent literature and on universities. Despite the all-encompassing title, numerous precise suggestions for future university involvement in world affairs are set forth. The committee was chaired by J. L. Morrill.

*39. Weidner, Edward W. *The World Role of Universities.* ("Carnegie Series on American Education.")

New York: McGraw-Hill Book Co., Inc., 1962. Pp. 366.

This book distinguishes itself by drawing the many university activities into a coherent whole. Of special importance are the several chapters discussing the expanding role of universities in technical assistance programs. Numerous recommendations, a methodological appendix, and a bibliography are included.

40. Wilson, Howard E. *American College Life as Education in World Outlook.* Prepared for the Carnegie Endowment for International Peace. Washington, D.C.: American Council on Education, 1956. Pp. 195.

The subject of this volume is "outside activities" in the education of college youth. Discussion focuses on (a) college life and its historical development, (b) physical facilities for informal learning, (c) college members as informal resources on world affairs, (d) student activities which influence the world view, (e) student travel as an educational experience, and (f) the means to better organization. The author's thesis is that

> . . . only as the manifold activities and influences of the campus may be interrelated to provide unity, coordinated to avoid conflict and duplication, and focused on objectives of international understanding . . . /that/ are worthy of educated men and women, can the life of the institution reach its highest level.

41. _____. "Pressures on Higher Education from America's International Responsibilities," *Pressures and Priorities in Higher Education: Current Issues in Higher Education*, 1965. Ed. G. Kerry Smith. Proceedings, 20th Annual National Conference on Higher Education, Association of Higher Education, Chicago, March 7-10, 1965, pp. 76-79.

Several pressures are noted: the pressure to broaden language study, the pressure to develop curricula in international relations, the pressure of government requests for personnel, and the pressure of planning for overseas contract programs.

*42. _____, and Wilson, Florence H. *American Higher Education and World Affairs*. Washington, D.C.: American Council on Education, 1963. Pp. 158.

This volume offers an analysis of institutional policy and administrative organization. The authors plead for each institution to survey its resources and plan for future activity in world affairs. The book includes a survey of recent government programs and a bibliography.

PART II

CURRICULA

II

CHAPTER 2 — THE INTERNATIONAL CONTENT OF UNDERGRADUATE CURRICULA

43. Arndt, C. O. (comp.). <u>Programs and Projects for International Understanding; A Report</u>. Ed. Lawrence Conrad. Oneonta, N.Y.: American Association of Colleges for Teacher Education, 1956. Pp. 160.

    The Association requested that its members submit information on successful projects and total programs in the international field; the responses included in this book are generally brief. A variety of curricular and extracurricular practices are described and a listing of organizations and agencies involved in international education is included.

*44. Bidwell, Percy Wells. "Foreign Affairs in the Colleges," <u>Journal of Higher Education</u>, XXXV (November, 1964), 426-33.

    "American colleges and universities in general have failed to recognize their responsibility for developing a body of intelligent public opinion in this country in the field of foreign affairs." Five reasons are given to account for this failure:

    > (1) the inadequate secondary-school preparation of entering freshmen; (2) a lack of interest in foreign affairs among faculty as well as students; (3) the ethnocentric character of introductory courses in history and the social sciences; (4) low enrollments in courses dealing with foreign countries and international relations; and (5) the failure of the colleges to coordinate internally their activities in the field of international education.

*45. _____. Undergraduate Education in Foreign Affairs. New York: King's Crown Press, 1962. Pp. 215.

The author's concern is with general rather than specialized undergraduate education, and the focus is on those students who will not pursue careers in a related field. He has interviewed faculty members and administrators from some forty institutions. His numerous explicit recommendations suggest that general undergraduate education in foreign affairs is presently in need of far-reaching changes.

46. Bland, Sister Joan. "Teaching International Relations," National Catholic Education Association Bulletin, LVII (February, 1961), 16-24.

A bibliography is included.

47. Bowles, Chester. "Education for World Responsibility," Liberal Education, XLVIII (March, 1962), 60-67.

48. Buehrig, Edward H. "Implications for the Undergraduate Curriculum of the Growing Importance of International Affairs and the Mounting Need to Understand World Cultures," Goals for Higher Education in a Decade of Decision: Current Issues in Higher Education, 1961. Ed. G. Kerry Smith. Proceedings, 16th Annual National Conference on Higher Education, Association of Higher Education, pp. 153-56.

Professor Buehrig suggests that the humanities be given due emphasis in undergraduate courses dealing with international relations and area study.

> How the humanities cope with our predicament is perhaps more important in the long run than the preoccupation of the social sciences with the immediate problems of international relations, for the former will have the greater influence on our intellectual and moral fiber.

49. Cajoleas, Louis P. "International Understanding: A Theoretical Analysis of a Goal in Education," Teachers College Record, LX (January, 1960), 188-94.

To achieve an international understanding, the author suggests a view from three perspectives: understanding of the parts of the world, understanding of the relation of the parts, and understanding of the world as a whole. The word "understanding" has three related viewpoints: information about others, emotional identification with others' problems, and development of patterns of individual and group action. The author is trying to stimulate a re-examination of the educator's role in American society in view of an increasingly interdependent world.

50. Caldwell, Oliver J. "The Liberal Arts in a Revolutionary World," Higher Education, XIX (January, 1963), 3-6.

51. Carleton, William G. "Courses on Communism: The Urgency of History," Teachers College Record, LXV (January, 1964), 346-56.

52. Cohen, Maurice. "Toward a Basic Undergraduate Course in World Civilization," Liberal Education, LI (May, 1965), 209-20.

53. Cole, Fred. International Relations in Institutions of Higher Education in the South. Washington, D.C.: American Council on Education, 1958. Pp. 169.

A comparative analysis of international relations course offerings in higher education institutions of the South, including a cross section of all types of institutions. Data was obtained by questionnaires and personal interviews. The analyses are of quantity of departments, courses, faculty members, libraries, and other specialized resources, and of kinds of departmental affiliation, facilities, and personnel available for international relations instruction. A bibliography is included.

*54. The College and World Affairs. New Haven, Conn.: Committee on the College and World Affairs, Hazen Foundation, 1964. Pp. 74. Available from Education and World Affairs.

The thesis is "that liberal learning must include study of the varying, constantly changing cultural conditions of men." The report suggests that the basic changes in world relations necessitate "a new intellectual outlook and that this profoundly different outlook requires a new strategy of liberal learning." This is one of the most significant treatments available on the subject. A bibliography is included. John W. Nason chaired the committee.

55. Education for International Understanding. Report on a project of the American Association of Colleges for Teacher Education. Plattsburg, N.Y.: State University College, 1963.

56. Ekman, Ernst. "Teaching of Scandinavian History in the U.S.," Scandinavian Studies, XXXVII (August, 1965), 259-70.

57. Forster, Kent. "A Pragmatic Program in General Education: The Penn State Course in International Understanding," Journal of Higher Education, XXXIV (October, 1963), 371-78.

The course was designed to introduce juniors and seniors majoring in the physical sciences to the complexity of the contemporary international scene. The article gives a detailed account of the problems that were faced at the outset and as the program evolved.

58. Garrison, Karl C. "Worldminded Attitudes of College Students in a Southern University," Journal of Social Psychology, LIV (1961), 147-53.

59. Ketcham, Ralph L. "An Evaluation of a General Education Course in World Affairs," Journal of General Education, XIV (April, 1962), 38-44.

60. Laves, Walter H. C. "International Understanding and Our Schools," American Association of Colleges for Teacher Education Yearbook. 9th Yearbook, Annual Meeting, Chicago, 1956, pp. 91-103.

*61. McClelland, Charles A. College Teaching of International Relations: Problems of Organization and Collaboration. San Francisco: Department of International Relations, San Francisco State College, 1962. Pp. 382.

The result of a three-year investigation, this volume reports on applied and experimental studies of undergraduate college education in international relations and on how an organized study of international relations can be made most effective. Components of the problem include: the teacher's skill and interests, the knowledge to be conveyed, the students' capabilities, and an evaluation of the results of teaching.

62. Morehouse, Ward. *The International Dimensions of Education in New York State*. Albany: University of the State of New York, 1963. Pp. 48.

63. Morgenthau, Hans J. "Education and World Politics," *Daedalus*, LXXXVIII (Winter, 1959), 121-38.

64. Murphy, Franklin D. "Languages and the National Interest," *Publications of the Modern Language Association*, LXXV (May, 1960), 25-29.

65. Niebuhr, Reinhold. "Education and the World Scene," *Daedalus*, LXXXVIII (Winter, 1959), 107-20.

66. Parker, William Riley. *The National Interest and Foreign Languages*. A Discussion Guide and Work Paper Prepared for Citizen Consultations Sponsored by the United States National Commission for UNESCO. ("U.S. Department of State Publication," No. 6389.) Washington, D.C.: National Commission for UNESCO, United States Department of State, 1957. Pp. 132.

    Bibliographies are included.

67. _____. "Why a Foreign Language Requirement?" *College and University*, XXXII (Winter, 1957), 189-203.

68. Redefer, Frederick L. "When Is Education International?" *Educational Forum*, XXVII (March, 1963), 261-66.

69. Swift, Richard N. *World Affairs and the College Curriculum*. Washington, D.C.: American Council on Education, 1959.

    This work reflects the concept that international relations can be best comprehended in the broad context of national histories and cultures and in the aspirations and achievements of their peoples. To achieve this understanding, an interdisciplinary approach to international relations is necessary. The author gives specific suggestions on how to broaden and improve course content, and on how to improve the major study.

70. Tead, Ordway. "Toward Worldmindedness in College Education," Teachers College Record, LXII (November, 1960), 133-37.

71. Tyrrell, William G. "Developing International Understanding in the First Two Years of College," Approaches to an Understanding of World Affairs. 25th Yearbook. Ed. Howard Richmond Anderson. Washington, D.C.: National Council for the Social Studies, 1954, pp. 383-95.

72. Wilson, Charles R. "The Ugly American Undergraduate," School and Society, XCII (November 28, 1964), 351-54.

73. Yalem, Ronald J. "Undergraduate Training in International Relations," Liberal Education, XLV (October, 1959), 398-404.

CHAPTER **3** THE INTERNATIONAL CONTENT OF TEACHER EDUCATION CURRICULA

74. American Education in a Revolutionary World: The Role of the States. Conference Report. Gould House, April 22-24, 1964. Albany: State Education Department, University of the State of New York, 1964. Pp. 32.

    Reviews what some states have done to bring the study of non-Western areas into the secondary school curricula.

75. Asian Studies in Undergraduate and Teacher Education. New York: Conference on Asian Affairs, Inc., 1955. Pp. 39.

    A bibliography is included.

76. Barker, H. Kenneth. "International Understanding and Teacher Education," Changes in Teacher Education: An Appraisal. Official Report, 18th National Commission on Teacher Education and Professional Standards Conference, June 25-28, 1963. Washington, D.C.: National Education Association, 1964, pp. 488-93.

77. _____. "Teacher Education for International Goals." (See No. 667.)

78. Bigelow, Karl W. "The Fourth Charles W. Hunt Lecture; Africa, Teacher Education, and the United States," American Association of Colleges for Teacher Education Yearbook. 16th Yearbook, Annual Meeting, 1963, pp. 102-12.

79. The Challenge of a Revolutionary World: Progress Report, 1964. Albany: State Education Department, University of the State of New York, 1964. Pp. 48.

80. Education for Freedom and World Understanding. (OE-10016.) A Report of the Working Committee of the Conference on the Ideals of American Freedom and the International Dimensions of Education, March 26-28, 1962. Washington, D.C.: Office of Education, United States Department of Health, Education and Welfare, 1962. Pp. 62.

81. Garrison, Karl C. "A Comparison of World-Minded Attitudes of Georgia and Oregon School Teachers," Journal of Teacher Education, XIV (June, 1963), 151-53.

82. McGee, Gale W. "World Responsibilities and the Education of Teachers," American Association of Colleges for Teacher Education Yearbook. 14th Yearbook, Annual Meeting, Chicago, 1961, pp. 65-74.

83. Stamm, Ester F. "Knowledge of World Affairs: A Requirement for Teachers?" Journal of Teacher Education, XIII (March, 1962), 39-46.

*84. Teacher and Curriculum. Report of the Conference on American Education in a Revolutionary World. Sponsored by the United States National Commission for UNESCO and the New York State Education Department. Washington, D.C.: The Commission, 1964. Pp. 76.

Thirteen papers view the problems and prospects of introducing the many cultures and societies of the world into the curricula at the primary and secondary school levels. Principal attention is given to the role of the states, teacher education, and curricular organization. A concluding essay provides a blueprint for action.

85. Welty, Paul S. "The World Challenge for Teacher Education," Teacher Education, Direction for the Sixties. Report, 10th Biennial School for Executives, Bemidji State College, Bemidji, Minn., August 21-27, 1960. Washington, D.C.: American Association of Colleges for Teacher Education, 1961, pp. 77-81.

86. Wilson, Howard E. "What Institutions of Higher Education Are Doing in Their Teaching and Activity Programs," Educational Record, XXXVII (April, 1956), 107-11.

CHAPTER **4** AREA STUDIES

PHILOSOPHY AND GENERAL DISCUSSION

87. American Education in a Revolutionary World: The Role of the States. (See No. 74.)

88. "Area Studies and the Library," Library Quarterly, XXXV (October, 1965), entire issue.

89. Armajani, Yahya. "Four College Area Studies: A Cooperative Program in the Understanding of Other Cultures," Association of American Colleges Bulletin, XLIII (March, 1957), 14-22.

   Name of Bulletin changed to Liberal Education beginning with Vol. XLV.

90. Axelrod, Joseph, and Bigelow, Donald N. Resources for Language and Area Studies. A Report on an Inventory of the Language Area Centers Supported by the National Defense Education Act of 1958. Washington, D.C.: American Council on Education, 1962. Pp. 96.

   At the request of the United States Office of Education, the American Council on Education has made a descriptive study of the forty-six language and area study centers which arose with the assistance of funds from the National Defense Education Act of 1958. Information was gathered in order to ascertain how the centers were organized, the number of students enrolled in language and area-study programs, the language-teaching methods used, and the coordination between language and area-studies curricula. Especially provocative is a chapter on the likely future course of these centers.

91. Bailey, Jackson H. "Non-Western Studies in the Small Liberal Arts College: An Experiment at Earlham and Antioch," <u>Liberal Education</u>, XLVII (October, 1961), 405-11.

92. Beckmann, George M. "Guidelines for an Experimental Curriculum with Major Emphasis on Non-Western Cultures," <u>Undergraduate Education: Current Issues in Higher Education, 1964</u>. Ed. G. Kerry Smith. Proceedings, 19th Annual Conference on Higher Education, American Association for Higher Education, April 19-22, 1964, pp. 168-71.

93. Bigelow, Donald N. "Backdoor to the Future," <u>Liberal Education</u>, XLIX (December, 1963), 481-87.

*94. _____, and Legters, Lyman H. <u>NDEA Language and Area Centers: Report on the First 5 Years</u>. (OE-56016.) Washington, D.C.: Office of Education, United States Department of Health, Education and Welfare, 1964. Pp. 131.

Discusses the growth, impact, and likely future development of NDEA programs.

*95. _____, and _____ (eds.). "The Non-Western World in Higher Education," <u>The Annals</u>, CCCLVI (November, 1964), entire issue.

Attempts are made to analyze the growth and chart the future course of non-Western studies: "The Leadership of the Universities," George E. Taylor; "The Role of the Foundations," George M. Beckmann; "The Federal Government and the Universities," Kenneth W. Mildenberger; "The Social Sciences in Non-Western Studies," Milton B. Singer; "The Humanities and Non-Western Studies," Albert H. Marckwardt; "South Asian Studies: A History," W. Norman Brown; "East Asian Studies: A Comprehensive Program," William Theodore de Bary; "Southeast Asia: An Economist's Viewpoint," Frank H. Golay; "Language Study and the Middle East," Charles A. Ferguson; "Uralic and Altaic: The Neglected Area," Denis Sinor; "Area Studies: Russia and Eastern Europe," Henry L. Roberts; "The Interdisciplinary Effect in African Studies," Conrad C. Reining; "The Strange Career of Latin American Studies," Richard M. Morse; "Instruction in

Chinese and Japanese in the Secondary Schools," Frederick H. Jackson; "Provincialism and Constitutionalism: The Role of the States," Ward Morehouse; "Development of Library Resources," Paul L. Berry; "International Study at Home and Abroad," Stephen A. Freeman.

96. Blackton, Charles S. "Undergraduate Area Studies in American Education," Journal of General Education, XII (July, 1959), 158-63.

    This article describes the Colgate undergraduate interdisciplinary area-studies courses and several alternatives to the Colgate program as practiced by other institutions.

97. Byrnes, Robert F. (ed.). The Non-Western Areas in Undergraduate Education in Indiana. ("Slavic and East Europe Series," No. 15.) Bloomington: Indiana University, 1959. Pp. 106.

    The essays summarize a 1958 survey of undergraduate instruction in non-Western areas at colleges and universities in Indiana. The unique value of this volume lies in the exposition of a statewide effort to communicate, coordinate, and eventually alter, curricular content to meet modern demands of world affairs education.

98. _____. "Teaching Materials for Foreign Area Instruction." (See No. 667.)

99. Caldwell, Oliver J. "Some Comments on Possible Experimental Curricula with Major Emphasis on Non-Western Cultures," Undergraduate Education: Current Issues in Higher Education, 1964. Ed. G. Kerry Smith. Proceedings, 19th Annual Conference on Higher Education, American Association for Higher Education, April 19-22, 1964, pp. 172-76.

100. The Challenge of a Revolutionary World: Progress Report, 1964. (See No. 79.)

101. Dean, Vera Micheles. The American Student and the Non-Western World. Cambridge, Mass.: Harvard University Press, 1956. Pp. 28.

     Mrs. Dean offers a deceptively simple argument for introducing studies of the non-Western world into our high schools and colleges. Following her "philosophy of necessity," she suggests an eight-point remedial program, the core of which is "the establishment of a small Institute for Non-Western Training where young men and women college graduates could be prepared to train students in schools, colleges, and other institutions."

*102. deBary, William Theodore. "Education for a World Community," Liberal Education, L (December, 1964), 437-57.

This article is filled with suggestions for the future course of non-Western studies. The general theme is that the new curricula must be fit into the traditional concept of liberal education.

103. "Developing Cultural Understanding Through Foreign Language Study: A Report of the MLA Interdisciplinary Seminar in Language and Culture," Publications of the Modern Language Association, LXVIII (December, 1953), 1, 196-218.

104. Fife, Austin E., and Nielsen, Marion L. (eds.). Conference on Neglected Languages; A Report. Washington, D.C.: March 27-28, 1961. New York: Modern Language Association of America, 1961. Pp. 7.

105. Flapan, Maxwell. "The World We Have to Know," American Education, I (October, 1965), 30-32.

American Education replaces Higher Education and School Life.

106. Gibb, Sir Hamilton Alexander Roskeen. Area Studies Reconsidered. London: School of Oriental and African Studies, University of London, 1963.

107. Hamar, Clifford E. "Two Articles from Last December," Liberal Education, LI (October, 1965), 404-12.

The author analyzes "Education for a World Community" by Theodore deBary (see No. 102) in terms of "The Threefold Cycle of Liberal Education" by Charles Virtue.

108. Hamilton, D. Lee. "Modern Foreign Languages and NDEA, Title VI," <u>Higher Education</u>, XIX (July, 1963), 3-8.

109. Henderson, Dan Fenno. <u>International Legal Studies and University Foreign Area Studies in Teaching of International Law and Related Courses in American Law Schools.</u> ("ASIL Occasional Paper.") Report of a Conference under the auspices of the American Society of International Law at Cornell Law School, June 21-24, 1964. Washington, D.C.: American Society of International Law, 1964.

110. Legters, Lyman H. "NDEA Support for Undergraduate Language and Area Studies," <u>Liberal Education</u>, LI (May, 1965), 278-83.

    Reviews the history of NDEA support for undergraduate study and announces thirty new institutions which will augment the former fifty-five NDEA centers.

111. _____. "The Overseas Dimension of the NDEA Language and Area Centers Program," <u>Educational Record</u>, XLVII (Winter, 1966), 57-62.

112. Lewis, Martin Deming. "How Many Histories Should We Teach?--Asia and Africa in a Liberal Arts Education," <u>Liberal Education</u>, XLVIII (October, 1962), 357-65.

113. McNiff, Phillip J. "Foreign Area Studies and Their Effect on Library Development," <u>College and Research Libraries</u>, XXIV (July, 1963), 291-96.

114. Mandelbaum, David Goodman, Lasker, Gabriel W., and Albert, Ethel M. (eds.) <u>The Teaching of Anthropology</u>. ("Memoirs," No. 94.) Menasha, Wis.: Anthropological Association, 1963. Pp. 611.

    A paper by John W. Bennett, "A Course in Comparative Civilizations," describes a proposed course for introducing freshmen to non-Western areas, as well as to cultural anthropology. McKim Marriott, in "An Indian Civilization Course," describes the interdisciplinary course at Chicago University designed especially for juniors.

115. Marron, James M., Tierney, Hannelore, and Dersham, James F. <u>Modern Foreign Language Enrollments in Higher Education: Junior Colleges, Four-Year Colleges, and Universities, Fall, 1963</u>. New York: Modern Language Association of America, 1964. Pp. 43.

116. Melady, Thomas P. "Needed: Afro-Asian Studies," <u>America</u>, CXII (May 15, 1965), 709-10.

   The president of the Africa Service Institute asks, "Will our diplomats and businessmen be able to deal with the non-Western world?"

117. Morehouse, Ward. "Adding a New Dimension to Liberal Education," <u>Liberal Education</u>, XLVI (October, 1960), 380-87.

*118. _____ (ed.). <u>Foreign Area Studies and the College Library</u>. ("Occasional Publication," No. 1.) New York: Foreign Area Materials Center, University of the State of New York, 1965. Pp. 73.

   Discussing bibliographies, reference service, acquisitions programs, and other activities and services for undergraduate librarians in African, Asian, Latin American, and Russian studies, the following papers are included: "Resources and Reference Services for Studies on Russia and the Soviet Union," Eleanor Buist; "Bibliographical Services on Tropical Africa: Resources and Prospects," Alfonso A. Castagno; "Latin American Bibliography: Recent and Current Activities in the United States," Howard F. Cline; "East Asian Studies and Library Resources: A Far-Eastern Scholar Looks at the Library," Hyman Kublin.

119. _____. "Foreign Area Studies in New York Schools and Colleges," <u>School and Society</u>, XCI (October 5, 1963), 280-82.

120. _____. "What Should Be the Role of Area Programs in the '60's?," <u>Platform for Higher Education; Guidelines for the Sixties: Current Issues in Higher Education, 1960</u>. Ed. G. Kerry Smith. Proceedings, 15th Annual National Conference on Higher Education, Association for Higher Education, Chicago, March 6-9, 1960, pp. 190-93.

The Educational Director of the Asia Society believes that the major role of area-study programs should be to train nonacademic specialists in foreign areas. He predicts that area-study programs are "going to be less useful in the years ahead in training for academic careers." In order to increase knowledge of non-Western areas, an effort must be made to universalize existing disciplines and promote the interdisciplinary study of foreign areas.

121. Morton, Louis. "National Security and Area Studies: The Intellectual Responses to the Cold War," Journal of Higher Education, XXXIV (March, 1963), 142-47.

One example of university response to increased United States participation in world affairs has been the birth and growth of area-studies programs. The objectives of such programs should be (a) to expand scholarly research on the area by increasing the body of experts, and (b) to provide specialized training for future government officials.

122. Moses, Larry (comp.). Language and Area Study Programs in American Universities. (See No. 838.)

*123. Non-Western Studies in the Liberal Arts College. Washington, D.C.: Commission on International Understanding, Association of American Colleges, 1964. Pp. 362.

Commissioned by the United States Office of Education, this report is a careful study of the curricular facilities on non-Western areas in America's liberal arts colleges. Alternative approaches are suggested, and numerous guidelines for program expansion and improvement are offered. Individual reports from a number of colleges and statistical appendices are included.

124. Palmer, Archie M., and Kruzas, Anthony T. (eds.). Research Centers Directory. 2nd ed. Detroit: Gale Research Co., 1965.

The directory lists and briefly describes regional and area-studies programs at United States institutions of higher education.

125. Reed, Howard A. "Intercultural or Non-Western Studies in General Education" in *General Education: Current Ideas and Concerns*. Ed. James G. Rice. Washington, D.C.: American Association for Higher Education, 1964. Also in *College and University Bulletin*, XVII (October 15, 1964), 2, 5-6.

126. _____. "Trends in Non-Western Studies in U.S. Liberal Arts Colleges," *Undergraduate Education: Current Issues in Higher Education, 1964*. Ed. G. Kerry Smith. Proceedings, 19th Annual Conference on Higher Education, American Association for Higher Education, April 19-22, 1964, pp. 177-79.

127. "Regional Associates Survey of Non-Western Material in the Undergraduate Curriculum," *ACLS Newsletter*, XII (September, 1961), 3-18.

128. *Report on a Cooperative Undergraduate Program for Critical Languages*. Princeton, N.J.: Princeton University, 1963. Pp. 17.

129. Rhoades, Margaret M. (comp.). *Research Centers on the Developing Areas*. (See No. 843.)

130. Sayres, William C. *The Non-Western World in New York State Higher Education*. Albany: Division of Research in Higher Education, University of the State of New York, 1961. Pp. 63.

    State survey of college courses on the Soviet Union, Asia, Africa, and Latin America.

131. Singer, Milton B., *et al*. "Chicago's Non-Western Civilizations Program," *Journal of General Education*, XII (January, 1959), 22-49.

132. Teichert, Pedro C. M. "The Importance of Foreign Area Studies," *Journal of Higher Education*, XXIX (January, 1958), 23-30.

    The author pleads for increased use of area-study instruction and uses Latin American economics as a case study. He calls for an increased degree of area specialization, which he claims is actually "despecialization" because it broadens the institutional outlook limited only to Western models and permits an interdisciplinary approach that is essential to a successful program. The author outlines what he considers to be an ideal course of study in Latin American economics.

133. Undergraduate Instruction in Critical Languages and Area Studies; Recommendations and Report. Conference on Undergraduate Instruction in Critical Languages, Princeton University, October 12-13, 1964. Princeton, N.J.: Princeton University, 1965. Pp. 32.

134. Ward, F. Champion. "What Did Confucius Say?: Animadversions on the Tribal Curriculum," Journal of General Education, XI (January, 1958), 3-6.

135. Whitaker, Urban. "An Application of Area Studies to the Teaching of General Education Courses in International Education," International Review of Education (Federal Republic of Germany, Hamburg), Vol. 4 (1959), 425-40.

AFRICA

136. "African Studies in the United States," African Studies Bulletin, IV,4 (May, 1961), 9-20.

137. Armstrong, Robert G. "The Role of Linguistics in African Studies," Phylon, XXV (Summer, 1964), 135-45.

138. Bordie, John G. (ed.). National Conference on the Teaching of African Languages and Area Studies. Washington, D.C.: Georgetown University, 1960. Pp. 63.

    Sponsored by the Office of Education, United States Department of Health, Education, and Welfare.

139. Davidson, Basil. "Wanted: A Library of African Classics," Africa Report (November, 1965), 24-28.

140. Reining, Conrad C. "The Interdisciplinary Effect in African Studies" in "The Non-Western World in Higher Education."(See No. 95.)

141. *Report on First Summer Program in African Languages, 1962.* East Lansing: African Language and Area Center, Michigan State University, 1962. Pp. 102.

142. United Nations Educational, Scientific and Cultural Organization. *Social Scientists Specializing in African Studies: Directory Prepared by the Secretariat of UNESCO.* Paris, Ecole Pratique des Hautes Etudes de l'Université de Paris, 1963. Pp. 375.

ASIA

143. Anderson, George L. "Cathay and the Way Thither: Oriental Literature in the World Literature Program," *Modern Language Journal*, XL (October, 1956), 316-18.

144. *Asian Studies in Undergraduate and Teacher Education.* (See No. 75.)

145. Beasley, William G. *Notes on the Teaching of Far Eastern History.* ("Teaching of History Leaflet," No. 20.) London: Published for the Historical Association by Routledge & Kegan Paul, 1962.

   The author offers a scheme for organizing the study of Japanese and Chinese history for British schools, advocating a description of traditional society and an account of the ways it has been forced to adjust to Western influences. A topical bibliography of materials is included.

146. Bingham, Woodbridge. "An Integrated Approach to an All-Asia Survey Course," *Association of American Colleges Bulletin*, XLIV (October, 1958), 408-15.

147. Boardman, Eugene Powers (ed.). *Asian Studies in Liberal Education; the Teaching of Asian History and Civilizations to Undergraduates.* Washington, D.C.: Association of American Colleges, 1959. Pp. 50.

AREA STUDIES

The papers discuss the organization and presentation of Asian Studies courses and programs on the undergraduate level at the following institutions: University of California at Berkeley, Harvard University, University of Chicago, Columbia College, and the University of Michigan.

148. Borton, Hugh. "Asian Studies and the American Colleges," Journal of Asian Studies, XVIII (November, 1958), 59-65.

149. Brown, W. Norman (ed.). Resources for South Asian Language Studies in the United States. Philadelphia: University of Pennsylvania Press, 1960. Pp. 103.

The eleven working papers and summary report of a conference convened by the University of Pennsylvania for the United States Office of Education, January 15-16, 1960. The participants represented almost all the universities in the United States where modern and classical South Asian languages are taught. Together they outline a program development agenda in the field. Information on what languages are taught, and where, is included.

150. _____. "South Asian Studies: A History" in "The Non-Western World in Higher Education." (See No. 95.)

151. Crane, Robert I. "The Role of the Introductory Asia Course in Undergraduate Education," Journal of General Education, XII (July, 1959), 164-69.

The University of Michigan's example provides excellent contrast with other programs primarily because the course encompasses a broad subject area. This article is important not only for its descriptive value but also for the arguments supporting the methods of instruction used and the organization of the course. Perhaps the most interesting aspect of the Michigan course is its emphasis on comparative methods in studying the civilizations of Asia.

152. Creel, Herrlee Glessner (ed.). Conference on Chinese Civilization in Liberal Education.

Chicago: University of Chicago, 1959. Pp. 222.

The proceedings of a conference at the University of Chicago in November, 1958; participants included some of the outstanding Sinologists in the country. The lengthy account consists of two formal papers and lively verbatim discussions on each of the following topics, all concerned with instruction on the undergraduate level: "The General Course on Chinese Civilization," "Chinese Art and Literature," "Chinese Philosophy and Religion," and "Chinese Political, Social, and Economic Institutions."

153. Danto, Arthur. "The Oriental Humanities and the Non-Orientalist," Journal of General Education, XII (January, 1959), 15-21.

154. deBary, William Theodore (ed.). Approaches to the Oriental Classics: Asian Literature and Thought in General Education. Report of the Conference on Oriental Classics in General Education, Columbia University, 1958. New York: Columbia University Press, 1960. Pp. 262.

Papers and proceedings from the Conference, September 12-13, 1958, include discussions of (a) the relation of Oriental literature to the purposes of education in the West and the place of this literature in the college curriculum, and (b) why certain books should be read and how they can best be presented in undergraduate education.

155. _____. "Asian Studies for Undergraduates: The Oriental Studies Program at Columbia College," Journal of Higher Education, XXX (January, 1959), 1-7.

156. _____. "East Asian Studies: A Comprehensive Program" in "The Non-Western World in Higher Education." (See No. 95.)

157. _____. "Oriental Classics in General Education," Journal of General Education, XII (January, 1959), 3-8.

*158. _____, and Embree, Ainslie (eds.). Approaches to Asian Civilizations. New York:

Columbia University Press, 1964. Pp. 293.

Thirty papers from the Conference on Oriental Civilizations in General Education at Columbia University, September 13-14, 1961, provide one of the most comprehensive volumes on this topic. In view of the instructor's problem of selecting essential material, "the judgment of specialists responsive to this great challenge . . . can be invaluable." Essays are grouped under the headings: history, politics, economics, anthropology and sociology, general, and organization of courses.

159. Echols, John M. "South East Asian Studies in the United States," United Asia, XI,5 (1959), 406-8.

160. Ehrman, Edith (ed.). "Guide to Asian Studies in Undergraduate Education," Association for Asian Studies: Newsletter, X, Suppl. No. 1 (September, 1964). Pp. 43.

161. Fairbank, John K. "A Note of Ambiguity: Asian Studies in America," Journal of Asian Studies, XIX (November, 1959), 3-9.

162. Frenz, Horst, and Anderson, George L. (eds.). Indiana University Conference on Oriental-Western Literary and Cultural Relations. 1st Conference, Indiana University, 1954. Chapel Hill: University of North Carolina Press, 1955. Pp. 241.

163. Golay, Frank H. "Southeast Asia: An Economist's Viewpoint" in "The Non-Western World in Higher Education." (See No. 95.)

164. Hallo, William W. "The Place of Oriental Studies in a University Curriculum," Journal of Higher Education, XXVII (January, 1956), 11-16.

165. Hartwell, Robert. "Teaching of Literary Chinese; Its Importance to the Social Scientist," Journal of Higher Education, XXXV (November, 1964), 434-41.

*166. Lambert, Richard D. (ed.). Resources for South Asian Area Studies in the United States. Report of the Conference on the Strengthening and Integration of South Asian Language and Area Studies. Philadelphia: University of Pennsylvania Press, 1962. Pp. 320.

For this collection of twenty-one conference working papers, the editor provides a convenient conclusion, summarizing the papers and conference proceedings.

167. Langlois, Walter G. "An Honors Program and the Growth of Asian Studies: The Asian Honors Seminar at Boston College," Journal of Higher Education, XXXIII (May, 1962), 237-43.

This article describes the problems and successes of beginning an Asian Studies program at a small college. The initial venture was an introduction to the culture via literature. Though the subject matter varied widely and integration of material was not stressed, the objective of grappling with unaccustomed material and breaking prejudices was accomplished.

168. Liu, James T. C. "An Orientation Course on Asian Civilizations," Journal of General Education, X (October, 1957), 228-35.

169. Marriott, McKim. "An Indian Civilization Course" in The Teaching of Anthropology. Ed. Mandelbaum, Lasker, and Albert. (See No. 114.)

170. Morehouse, Ward (ed.). Asian Studies in Liberal Arts Colleges. Washington, D.C.: Association of American Colleges, 1961. Pp. 48.

Papers prepared for a session on "Asian Studies in Liberal Arts Colleges," at the annual meeting of the Association for Asian Studies at Chicago, March, 1961.

171. _____. "Asian Studies in Undergraduate Education," Journal of General Education, XI (July, 1958), 125-40.

172. _____. "The Pinebrook Experiment," Liberal Education, L (December, 1964), 526-36.

"A non-Western Pugwash /is/ appraised by the Conference director."

AREA STUDIES 39

173. Robbins, John. "The New Asia and American Education," *Teachers College Record*, LXII (February, 1961), 339-47.

174. Singer, Milton B. (ed.). *Introducing India in Liberal Education*. Chicago: University of Chicago, 1957. Pp. 287.

   This comprehensive treatment of Indian studies also provides suggestions for the teaching of courses on other areas. The conference for which these papers and session summaries were prepared was organized under four headings: Indian civilization as the unit of course organization, the changing dimensions of Indian society, forms of cultural expression, collections of readings and methods of teaching. Bibliographies are included on village India, India as a culture area, Indo-Anglian literature, and Indian social institutions.

*175. Teng, S. Y. (ed.). *Asian Studies and State Universities*. Bloomington: Indiana University, 1960. Pp. 138.

   The proceedings of a conference on Asian Studies held at Indiana University, November 11-13, 1959. This volume includes addresses and discussion on (a) the importance of Asian Studies in American higher education, (b) the obligations of larger institutions with respect to Asian Studies, (c) the relation of Asian Studies to traditional academic disciplines, (d) opportunities for smaller colleges in the field of Asian Studies, (e) Asian Studies and national security, (f) implementing a program of Asian Studies: practical problems and their solutions. A summary essay concludes the volume. Appendixes include an essay on "Asian Studies in America: A Historical Survey" and a bibliography titled, "Basic Recent English Books on Asia for College Libraries."

176. Van Neil, Robert. "Southeast Asian Studies in the U.S.A.," *Journal of Southeast Asian History*, V (March, 1964), 188-94.

177. Weiner, Myron. "The Study of Indian Civilization at the University of Chicago: Needs and Choices," *Journal of General Education*, XII (January, 1959), 24-28.

The article explains the origin, structure, and problems of conducting a general education course on Indian Civilization at the University of Chicago. The one-year course is oriented toward specific questions. It is not designed for specialists but is intended to be a part of the student's basic education in his third year.

178. Wright, Arthur F. "Chinese History for the Undergraduate," Journal of General Education, XIV (July, 1962), 93-102.

LATIN AMERICA

179. Bumgartner, Louis E. "The Shotgun Approach to Latin America," South Atlantic Quarterly, LXIV (Spring, 1965), 188-93.

180. Cline, Howard F. (ed.). Latin American Studies in the United States. Washington, D.C.: Hispanic Foundation, Reference Department, Library of Congress, 1958. Pp. 115.

    Proceedings of a meeting held in Chicago, November 6-8, 1958, under the joint auspices of the American Council of Learned Societies and the Newberry Library, assisted by the Hispanic Foundation. Working and related papers are included.

181. Guide to Latin American Studies. Los Angeles: Latin American Center, UCLA, 1966. Pp. 500.

182. Johnson, Harvey L. "Latin American Area Programs," Hispania, XLIV (May, 1961), 304-7.

183. Kling, Merle. "Area Studies and Comparative Politics," American Behavioral Scientist, VIII (September, 1964), 7-11.

    The history, accomplishments, and future of comparative political research on Latin America are discussed. A bibliography is included.

184. Meyer, Samuel L., and Cullen, Arthur J. "A Spanish-Speaking College in North America;

AREA STUDIES

A 'Prospectus' of a Unique Venture in Inter-American Education," <u>Liberal Education</u>, XLIX (May, 1963), 218-25.

185. Morse, Richard M. "The Strange Career of Latin American Studies" in "The Non-Western World in Higher Education." (See No. 95.)

MIDDLE EAST

186. Ferguson, Charles A. "Language Study and the Middle East" in "The Non-Western World in Higher Education." (See No. 95.)

187. Halpern, Manfred. "Middle Eastern Studies; A Review of the State of the Field with a Few Examples," <u>World Politics</u>, XV (October, 1962), 108-22.

188. Hodgson, Marshall. "A Non-Western Civilization Course in a Liberal Education with Special Attention to the Case of Islam," <u>Journal of General Education</u>, XII (January, 1959), 39-49.

189. Hurewitz, Jacob C. "Undergraduate Foreign Area Studies: The Case of the Middle East," Report on a Conference at Gould House, Dobbs Ferry, N.Y., March 6-7, 1964, <u>ACLS Newsletter</u>, XV (April, 1964), 1-15.

190. _____. <u>Undergraduate Instruction on the Middle East in American Colleges and Universities</u> (Provisional draft). New York: American Association for Middle East Studies, 1962. Pp. 80.

RUSSIA AND EASTERN EUROPE

191. Black, Cyril E., and Thompson, John M. (eds.). <u>American Teaching About Russia</u>. Bloomington: Indiana University Press, 1959. Pp. 189.

The three papers presented are a distillation of papers and proceedings of three separate conferences that dealt with secondary, undergraduate, and graduate instruction in Russian area studies. "The Study of Russia in Secondary Education" by George Barr Carson, Jr., emerged from a meeting of Russian-studies scholars and leaders in secondary education. A study of Russian and other non-Western area course offerings in Indiana colleges and universities provided data for "Russia and Other Non-Western Areas in Undergraduate Education" by Robert F. Byrnes and John M. Thompson. "Graduate Study of Russia" by Cyril E. Black and John M. Thompson was based on an intensive study of the leading American universities involved in the field.

192. Byrnes, Robert F. (ed.). "Reflections on American Training Programs on Russia," with comments by Cyril E. Black and George E. Taylor, Slavic Review, XXVII (September, 1962), 487-99.

193. _____, and Thompson, John M. "Undergraduate Study of Russia and the Non-Western World," Liberal Education, XLV (May, 1959), 268-83.

194. Fisher, Harold H. "Growing Pains of Slavic and East European Area Training," American Slavic and East European Review, XVII (October, 1958), 346-50.

195. Manning, Clarence A. A History of Slavic Studies in the United States. ("Marquette Slavic Studies," No. 3.) Milwaukee, Wis.: Marquette University, 1957. Pp. 117.

A bibliography is included.

196. Morehouse, Ward. "Strengthening the Study of Neglected Cultures: The Columbia University Seminar on Russian Literature," Journal of Higher Education, XXXIV (June, 1963), 311-17.

197. Mosely, Philip E. "The Growth of Russian Studies" in American Research on Russia. Ed. Harold Henry Fisher. Bloomington: Indiana University Press, 1959, pp. 1-22.

198. Roberts, Henry L. "Area Studies: Russia and Eastern Europe" in "The Non-Western World in Higher Education." (See No. 95.)

CHAPTER 5 TRAINING FOR INTERNATIONAL SERVICE

GENERAL

199. The American Overseas. Hearings before the Committee on Foreign Relations, United States Senate. (86th Cong. 1st sess.) With a statement by Harlan Cleveland. Washington, D.C.: Government Printing Office, 1959. Pp. 48.

*200. Arensberg, Conrad Maynadier, and Niehoff, Arthur H. Introducing Social Change; A Manual for Americans Overseas. Chicago: Aldine Publishing Co., 1964. Pp. 214.

   Discusses the concept of culture, planned changes, characteristics of the developing areas, American cultural values, and problems of work in the field.

201. Barnett, Vincent M., Jr. "Changing Problems of United States Representatives Abroad," Public Administration Review, XVII (Winter, 1957), 20-30.

202. _____ (ed.). The Representation of the United States Abroad. Rev. ed. New York: Published for the American Assembly by Frederick A. Praeger, Publishers, 1965. Pp. 251.

203. Barton, R. D. "Global Careers: A Program," Overseas, I (January, 1962), 7-10.

   An explanation of the Columbia University program designed to make training in international relations a part of the student's specialized graduate and professional education. The course, titled "The Role of the U.S. in World Affairs," tries to avoid both the introductory survey and advanced types of course instruction. Recruitment is limited to American men admitted to a graduate degree program and intending to pursue careers related to international affairs.

204. Bigelow, Karl W. "Teachers for Africa," Overseas, III (November, 1963), 18-22.

205. Buitron, Anibal. "Working Relations with National and Local Officials in Technical Assistance Programmes," Economic Development and Cultural Change, II (January, 1954), 279-85.

206. Byrnes, Francis C. Americans in Technical Assistance: A Study of Attitudes and Responses to Their Role Abroad. ("Praeger Special Studies in Economics and Development.") New York: Frederick A. Praeger, Publishers, 1965. Pp. 156.

207. Caldwell, Lynton K. "The Role of the Technical Expert," The Annals, CCCXXIII (May, 1959), 91-99.

208. Cleveland, Harlan, and Mangone, Gerard J. (eds.). The Art of Overseasmanship. Syracuse, N.Y.: Syracuse University Press, 1957. Pp. 150.

Papers presented at the Conference on Americans at Work Abroad, sponsored by the Maxwell School of Citizenship and Public Affairs, Syracuse University, March, 1957. The contributors point out several factors which facilitate successful work overseas.

*209. _____, _____, and Adams, John Clarke. The Overseas Americans. 1st ed. New York: McGraw-Hill Book Co., Inc., 1960. Pp. 316.

In this study of education for civilian Americans in overseas service, four main questions are asked: (a) What are the unique factors involved in working abroad? (b) To what extent are these factors presently considered in the education and training of those planning to go abroad? (c) What is being done to prepare civilians for service abroad? (d) What should be done? Information was gathered from interviews and personality tests of 244 United

States citizens and interviews with 200 foreign nationals in six countries: Mexico, Yugoslavia, Ethiopia, Iran, Indonesia, and Japan.

210. _____, _____, and _____. "The Overseas Americans: Agenda for Action," Institute of International Education: News Bulletin, XXXV (March, 1960), 13-21. Reprinted from The Overseas Americans. New York: McGraw-Hill Book Co., Inc., 1960.

211. Dustan, Jane. Training American Businessmen for Work Abroad. 2nd ed. New York: Council for International Progress in Management, U.S.A., 1961. Pp. 36.

*212. Esman, Milton J. Needed: An Education and Research Base to Support America's Expanded Commitments Overseas. Pittsburgh: University of Pittsburgh Press, 1961. Pp. 46.

This monograph examines the educational policies, institutions, and practices needed to provide the personnel for growing United States activity overseas. Everyone involved in these operations should understand his role as a United States representative, his role as an agent of social change, the social environment of his host society, and the ways he may act meaningfully in that environment. Proper personnel training demands a great deal more inquiry to produce multidisciplinary knowledge about (a) pre-industrial societies, (b) processes of induced rapid social change, and (c) culture, values and behavior affecting cross-cultural operations. The author includes suggestions to maximize the present capacity of overseas personnel. The need for federal financing is explained.

213. Evans, P. C. C. "American Teachers for East Africa," Comparative Education Review, VI (June, 1962), 69-77.

214. Fairchild, Mildred L., and Wann, Kenneth D. "The Educational Consultant in Another Culture," Teachers College Record, LVII (April, 1956), 438-48.

215. Fayerweather, John. The Executive Overseas: Administrative Attitudes and Relationships in

a Foreign Culture. Syracuse, N.Y.: Syracuse University Press, 1959. Pp. 195.

216. Fuller, C. Dale. _Training of Specialists in International Relations_. Washington, D.C.: American Council on Education, 1957. Pp. 136.

The author describes and evaluates college and university graduate programs designed to educate specialists in international relations. Contents include:(a) a definition of the focus of international relations, (b) a characterization of the specialist, (c) a sketch of various programs, (d) an enumeration of the strengths and weaknesses of these programs as seen by former students, and (e) suggestions for improving instruction. The book is partially based on interviews with a number of former graduate students who are now pursuing their specialty in international relations, and with fifty-six government officials.

217. Gray, Jack D. _Exploratory Project in Orientation and In-Service Training for Overseas Service_. College Station, Tex.: Texas Agricultural and Mechanical College, in press.

218. Griffith, Ernest S. "The Challenge of International Education; Five Years of the School of International Service," _Journal of Higher Education_, XXXVI (January, 1965), 32-37.

An account of the progress of American University's School of International Service established in 1958. In view of the "education for occupation" orientation, the article provides interesting contrasts to the majority of international education efforts.

219. Hall, Edward T., Jr. "Orientation and Training in Government for Work Overseas," _Human Organization_, XV (Spring, 1956), 4-10.

220. _____, and Whyte, William Foote. "Intercultural Communication: A Guide to Men of Action," _Human Organization_, XIX (Spring, 1960), 5-12.

221. Howell, Margaret A., and Newman, Sidney H. "How Should We Train for Overseas Posts?" _Public Personnel Review_, XIX (April, 1958), 130-32.

Twenty-four officers draw on overseas duty experience to outline a desirable training program.

222. Humphrey, Richard A. "Overseas Assignment," Liberal Education, XLVIII (March, 1962), 71-76.

223. Mandell, Milton M. "Selecting Americans for Overseas Assignments," Personnel Administration (Washington, D.C.), XXI (November-December, 1958), 25-30.

224. Mangone, Gerard J. "How Can We Better Educate Americans to Work and to Study Abroad," Platform for Higher Education; Guidelines for the Sixties: Current Issues in Higher Education, 1960. Ed. G. Kerry Smith. Proceedings, 15th Annual National Conference on Higher Education, Association for Higher Education, Chicago, March 6-9, 1960, pp. 119-23.

The author explodes the following fallacies concerning representatives abroad: knowledge of a language is not all important, area expertise is not necessary, ingredients for an effective performance are constant no matter what the occupation, and the new academic discipline, "overseasmanship," should not exist. A seven-point outline for the education of Americans working abroad concludes the article: (a) The best recruiting program is one combined with training. (b) Universities must be primarily responsible for these programs. (c) The best training should include overseas experience. (d) Area study programs can be effective modes of introducing alien cultures and ideologies. (e) Professional schools need to recognize that many of their students will reside overseas. (f) Administrative processes at home and abroad should be stressed. (g) Training must include substantial information on the United States as well.

225. Masland, John Wesley, and Radway, Laurence I. Soldiers and Scholars: Military Education and National Policy. Princeton, N.J.: Princeton University Press, 1961. Pp. 530.

This study of United States military education

emphasizes the training of career officers involved in the formulation of national policy. An account of the events and processes which have involved these individuals in many non-military activities is followed by an enumeration of qualifications which these positions demand. The remainder of the book describes and analyzes the general (as opposed to special) education programs of the service colleges.

226. Montgomery, John D. "Crossing the Culture Bars; an Approach to the Training of American Technicians for Overseas Assignments," World Politics, XIII (July, 1961), 544-60.

227. Morgan, Theodore. "The Underdeveloped Area Expert: South Asia Model," Economic Development and Cultural Change, II (April, 1953), 27-31.

228. Personnel for the New Diplomacy: Report. Washington, D.C.: Committee on Foreign Affairs Personnel, Carnegie Endowment for International Peace, 1962. Pp. 161.

229. Peter, Hollis W., and Henry, Edwin R. "Measuring Successful Performance Overseas," International Development Review, III (October, 1961), 8-12.

230. Public Administration Clearing House. "Experience of Personnel of U.S. Voluntary Agencies," Economic Development and Cultural Change, II (June, 1954), 329-49.

231. Sanders, Irwin T. (ed.). Interprofessional Training Goals for Technical Assistance Personnel Abroad, Report. Interprofessional Conference on Training of Personnel for Overseas Service, Cornell University, 1959. New York: Council on Social Work Education, 1959. Pp. 198.

232. Sayre, Wallace S., and Thurber, Clarence E. Training for Specialized Mission Personnel. Chicago: Public Administration Clearing House, 1952. Pp. 85.

Though specific examples are dated, the thorough discussion of various aspects of training for overseas service is relevant to an increasing number of similar programs with which universities are involved, whether by government, foundation, or other contract.

233. Spector, Paul, and Preston, Harley O. *Working Effectively Overseas*. Prepared for the Peace Corps by the Institute for International Services of the American Institute for Research. Washington, D.C.: The Institute, 1961.

234. Stalker, John N. "Peace Corps Training for Businessmen," *Overseas*, III (March, 1964), 23-25.

235. Torre, Mottram (ed.). *The Selection of Personnel for International Service*. A Project of the World Federation for Mental Health. New York: The Federation, 1963. Pp. 161.

A bibliography is included.

236. *Training of Foreign Affairs Personnel*. Hearings before the Committee on Foreign Relations, United States Senate (88th Cong., 1st sess.). Washington, D.C.: Government Printing Office, 1963. Pp. 492.

237. Wengert, Egbert S. "Can We Train for 'Overseasmanship'?" Review of *The Art of Overseasmanship*, ed. Harlan Cleveland and Gerard J. Mangone (see No. 206), in *Public Administration Review*, XVIII (Spring, 1958), 136-39.

238. Willner, A. R. "The Foreign Expert in Indonesia: Problems of Adjustability and Contribution," *Economic Development and Cultural Change*, II (April, 1953), 71-80.

239. *Working Abroad: A Discussion of Psychological Attitudes and Adaptation in New Situations*. (Report No. 41.) New York: Committee on International Relations, Group for the Advancement of Psychiatry, 1958.

PEACE CORPS

240. Bush, Gerald W. "Peace Corps Training: Trials, Tribulations, Lessons," Educational Leadership, XXII (May, 1965), 577-79, 583.

    The Executive Secretary of the Peace Corps discusses the various components of Peace Corps education and lists the lessons of the early years.

241. Butts, R. Freeman. American Education in International Development. (See No. 754.)

242. Englund, David L. "Peace Corps Training and the American University," International Review of Education, XI, 2 (1965), 209-17.

*243. Fairfield, Roy P. "The Peace Corps and the University," Journal of Higher Education, XXXV (April, 1964), 189-201.

    This article asks several vital questions about university involvement in Peace Corps training. (a) Does federal control follow federal money? (b) What are the dangers of extending campus boundaries around the world? (c) Is "training" education? (d) What Peace Corps policies create problems for the university? (e) Are universities fully aware of the internal consequences of signing a Peace Corps or international contract? (f) Is status seeking involved in the motive? (g) How long will universities participate without getting recognition for their effort?

244. Finch, Rogers B. "The Peace Corps and Higher Education--Two Years of Partnership," Higher Education, XIX (June, 1963), 3-6, 26-27.

245. Fuller, William A., Jr. "A View of the Peace Corps," Educational Forum, XXX (November, 1965), 95-101.

246. Ginsberg, Mitchell I. "Short-Term Training for the Peace Corps," *Social Work*, IX (January, 1964), 62-68.

247. Hayes, Samuel Perkins. *An International Peace Corps: The Promise and Problems*. Washington, D.C.: Public Affairs Institute, 1961. Pp. 96.

*248. Iversen, Robert W. "Peace Corps Training: Lessons of the First Year," *Educational Record*, XLIV (January, 1963), 17-25.

The author reviews the nature of the job, trainee, training facilities, and training program and concludes with several suggestions for training program improvement: (a) Precise information is needed about the job to be performed. (b) An accurate statement should be made about the level of language competence required. (c) All phases of training must be well coordinated. (d) Varied programs should be provided for varying students. (e) The size of the training group should be between 50 and 100. (f) It is necessary to provide information on the daily environment. (g) The majority of future training must be conducted by established institutions. (h) Colleges and universities should consider preparing possible future candidates before formal training. (i) Training on the job should be required.

249. Kauffman, Joseph F. "A Report on the Peace Corps," *Journal of Higher Education*, XXXIII (October, 1962), 361-66.

250. Kittler, Glenn D. *The Peace Corps*. With an Introduction by R. Sargent Shriver. New York: Paperback Library, 1963. Pp. 127.

251. Madow, Pauline (ed.). *The Peace Corps*. (*The Reference Shelf*, XXXVI,2.) New York: H. W. Wilson Co., 1964. Pp. 172.

A bibliography is included.

252. Maretzki, T. "Transition Training: A Theoretical Approach," *Human Organization*, XXIV (Summer, 1965), 128-34.

253. Shaftel, F. R. "Peace Corps Teachers in Malaya," <u>Educational Leadership</u>, XXI (March, 1964), 347-51.

254. Shinagel, Michael. "Harvard Volunteers in the Peace Corps: The First Two Years," <u>Harvard Alumni Bulletin</u>, LXV (April, 1963), 509-14.

255. Smith, M. Brewster. "Explorations in Competence: A Study of Peace Corps Teachers in Ghana," <u>American Psychologist</u>, XXI (June, 1966).

256. _____, et al. "Factorial Study of Morale Among Peace Corps Teachers in Ghana." (See No. 494.)

257. Stone, Donald C. "The Peace Corps: Caveats," <u>Overseas</u>, I (December, 1961), 6-10.

258. Wingenbach, Charles E. <u>The Peace Corps: Who, How, and Where</u>. Rev. ed. With a Preface by R. Sargent Shriver and a Foreword by Hubert H. Humphrey. New York: John Day Co., 1963. Pp. 188.

PART III

EDUCATIONAL EXCHANGE

CHAPTER 6   GENERAL DISCUSSION OF EDUCATIONAL EXCHANGE

259. Barnett, Norman N. "AIESEC--A Growing International Student Exchange Program," Journal of College Placement, XXII (February, 1962), 40-41, 86.

    Description of a reciprocal on-the-job training program for students of business and economics.

260. Bier, Jesse. "The Full, Bright Experience; An End to Innocents Abroad," Journal of Higher Education, XXXI (November, 1960), 435-42.

    The author presents a stimulating comparison of the French and American systems of higher education and claims the over-all similarities outweigh the differences. Especially interesting is the analysis of the strengths and weaknesses of the French system.

261. Byrnes Robert F. "Academic Exchange with the Soviet Union," Russian Review, XXI (July, 1962), 213-25.

262. Cater, Douglass. World Progress Through Educational Exchange; The Story of a Conference. Report of the 3rd National Conference on Exchange of Persons, Washington, D.C., 1959. New York: Institute of International Education, 1959. Pp. 39.

*263. College and University Programs of Academic Exchange. New York: Committee on Educational Interchange Policy, Institute of International Education, 1960. Pp. 36.

    This pamphlet summarizes much of the literature in the field of academic exchange. In the form of searching questions, the pamphlet challenges universities to re-examine their programs in order to obtain maximum efficiency and benefits from them. Section headings include: "Foreign Students in the U.S.," "U.S. Students Abroad," "Foreign Faculty and Research Scholars," "U.S. Faculty Abroad," and "Short-Term Exchanges."

264. "Cross-Cultural Education and Educational Travel," *International Social Science Bulletin*, VIII,4 (1956), entire issue.

Essays included are: "Cross-Cultural Education and Cultural Change," M. Brewster Smith; "The Relation of Culture-Goals to the Mental Health of Students Abroad," Dallas Pratt; "The Statistics of Study Abroad," Allan J. A. Elliott; "The Philosophy of the Fulbright Programme," Donald B. Cook and J. Paul Smith; "Statistics and Comments on Exchange with the United States," Kenneth Holland; "Social Aspects of Educational Travel in Japan," J. Watanabe; "Some Examples of International Scholarship and Fellowship Programmes," Nicole J. Deney.

265. Dawes, Norman. *A Two-Way Street*. New York: Asia Publishing House, 1962. Pp. 180.

This book is written in praise of the Fulbright educational exchange program between the United States and India. In a light and often humorous manner, the author describes the administrative procedures involved and relates numerous cases of individual and project successes under the program.

266. "Educational Exchange for the Mutual Development of Nations," *Institute of International Education: News Bulletin*, XXXVI (December, 1960), entire issue.

This issue is devoted to information on educational conditions and international educational exchange activities in seven designated areas of the world: South and Southeast Asia, North Asia, Africa south of the Sahara, Middle East and North Africa, Latin America, Eastern Europe and the Soviet Union, Australia, Canada, New Zealand, and Western Europe.

267. Educational Exchange in the Atlantic Area. New York: Committee on Educational Interchange Policy, Institute of International Education, 1965. Pp. 36.

A bibliography is included.

268. Inter-American Exchange: A Search for Understanding. A Report on the Inter-American Seminar on Educational Travel Programs, Bogota, Colombia, January 21-25, 1962. New York: Council on Student Travel, 1962. Pp. 16.

269. International Educational and Cultural Exchange. Washington, D.C.: Advisory Commission on International Educational and Cultural Affairs, United States Department of State, quarterly.

First appearing in the Summer of 1965, this publication is intended to serve as a forum. "The Commission invites interested agencies and groups, government and private, to use this publication to fill the assumed need for a central forum for the expression of divergent views."

270. "International Exchanges of Trainees," International Labor Review, LXXV (March, 1957), 230-45.

271. Macgregor, Gordon, et al. The Exchange of Scholars with Countries of the Near East and South Asia: Report of the Problems Arising from Cross-Cultural Differences in the Fulbright Programs with India and Iraq. Submitted by the Advisory Committee for the Near East and South Asia to the Committee on International Exchange of Persons, Conference Board of Associated Research Councils, Washington, D.C.: The Board, 1955. Pp. 90.

*272. Melby, John F. (ed.). "The Rising Demand for International Education," The Annals, CCCXXXV (May, 1961), entire issue.

Essays on several aspects of educational exchange: "Why?" John F. Melby; "Who is He?" Kenneth Holland; "The First Fifteen Years of the Fulbright Program," J. William Fulbright; "The Two-Week Orientation Center Program," Forrest G. Moore and Clarke A. Chambers; "The Four-Week Mixed Program," George P. Springer; "The University of Hawaii Orientation Center," Sumie F. McCabe; "The Academic Performance of Foreign Students," Ivan Putnam, Jr.; "The Community's Role in Cross-Cultural Education," Katherine C. Bang; "Africa," Gordon P. Hagberg; "Asia," Robert Blum; "Europe," Edouard Morot-Sri; "Latin America," Joe W. Neal; "Middle East," Harold B. Minor; "Foreign Student Adviser: A New Profession?" James M. Davis; "The American Goes Abroad," Donald J. Shank; "What Others Are Doing," Oliver J. Caldwell; "The World Looks at the American Program," Charles H. Malik; "Cultural Communication and New Imperatives," Richard A. Humphrey; "Anatomy of the Problem: Who Should Come?," Elinor K. Wolf.

273. Report of a Task Force on "Exchange of Persons." (See No. 694.)

274. Report of the National Conference on Exchange of Persons. New York, Institute of International Education, annually.

Summaries of addresses and discussions make the Report a valuable resource on the topic.

275. Sharp, Paul F. "International Commitments of the American College," Liberal Education, L (October, 1964), 321-27.

The author calls for increased participation by American colleges in international educational exchange. Far more faculty members must go overseas, and the campus must admit many more foreign students. Now is the time to solve the problems of qualifications of foreign students, preparing an adequate curriculum to suit the students' needs, finances, and counseling.

276. Shimbori, Michiya. "International Exchange of Scholars," Educational Record, XLI (October, 1960), 312-18.

277. Speakman, Cummins E., Jr. International Exchange in Education. ("The Library of

Education Series.") New York: To be published for the Center for Applied Research in Education by Prentice-Hall, Inc., in press.

278. Stone, Donald C. "Some Research and Action Needs in International Educational Exchange," Educational Record, XXXIX (October, 1958), 374-81.

279. Storey, Robert G. "Exchanges in the Legal Profession," Institute of International Education: News Bulletin, XXXIII (October, 1957), 9-12.

280. Teacher and Scholar Abroad: First-Person Reports of the U.S. Exchange Program. Prepared by the Board of Foreign Scholarships. Washington, D.C.: Bureau of Educational and Cultural Affairs, United States Department of State, 1964.

   Largely quotations from United States and foreign students and teachers involved in the United States Educational Exchange Program of the Department of State. Includes comments from students on subjects of study projects, orientation programs, and mutual understanding. Teachers report on their orientation to overseas duties, problems of adjustment, and host reactions to them. Statistics on each exchange category are given.

281. Useem, John and Ruth H., and Donoghue, John. "Men in the Middle of the Third Culture: The Roles of American and Non-Western People in Cross-Cultural Administration," Human Organization, XXII (Fall, 1963), 169-79.

282. Viederman, Stephen. "Academic Exchange, A Narrow Bridge," Bulletin of the Atomic Scientists, XVIII (February, 1962), 17-21.

283. Young, Francis A. "The Fulbright Program in Asia," Items (Social Science Research Council), XV (September, 1961), 29-32.

284. _____. "International Exchanges of Teachers and Scholars: U.S.A.," Education and International Life. Yearbook of Education. New York: Harcourt, Brace & World, 1964.

CHAPTER **7** HISTORY OF EDUCATIONAL EXCHANGE

285. Brickman, William W. "The Meeting of East and West in Educational History," <u>Comparative Education Review</u>, V (October, 1961), 82-89.

286. Colligan, Francis J. <u>Twenty Years After: Two Decades of Government-Sponsored Cultural Relations</u>. ("United States Department of State Publication," No. 6689; "International Information and Cultural Series," No. 59.) Washington, D.C.: The Department, 1958. Pp. 20.

287. Cotner, Thomas E. <u>A Summary of the Exchange and Training Programs, Office of Education, United States Department of Health, Education and Welfare 1939-1964</u>. (See No. 664.)

288. <u>International Educational Exchange Program, 1948-1958</u>. (" United States Department of State Publication," No. 6710; "International Information and Cultural Series," No. 60.) Washington, D.C.: International Educational Exchange Service. The Department, 1958. Pp. 65.

289. McMurry, Ruth E., and Lee, Muna. <u>The Cultural Approach, Another Way in International Relations</u>. Chapel Hill: University of North Carolina Press, 1947. Pp. 280.

    Bibliographical references are included in "Notes," pp. 248-66.

290. Metraux, Guy S. <u>Exchange of Persons: The Evolution of Cross-Cultural Education</u>. New York: Social Science Research Council, 1952. Pp. 53.

HISTORY OF EDUCATIONAL EXCHANGE

A history of cross-cultural education from the earliest traveling students to the latest twentieth century developments with special attention to more recent trends, this monograph was a preliminary to research on cross-cultural education sponsored by the Social Science Research Council.

291. Nakaya, Kenichi, and Schwantes, Robert S. *Ten Years of Cultural and Educational Interchange Between Japan and America 1952-1961.* A Report submitted to the Joint United States-Japan Conference on Cultural and Educational Interchange. Washington, D.C.: Bureau of Educational and Cultural Affairs, United States Department of State, 1962.

292. Schwantes, Robert S. *Japanese and Americans: A Century of Cultural Relations.* New York: Published for the Council on Foreign Relations by Harper & Row, 1955. Pp. 380.

   There is a bibliographic essay, pp. 333-72.

293. *The Second Five Years: A Report on the Fulbright Programme in the United Kingdom and Dependent Territories, 1954-1959.* London: United States Educational Commission in the United Kingdom, 1960. Pp. 106.

294. *A Survey of Chinese Students in American Universities and Colleges in the Past One Hundred Years.* A Preliminary Report. Under the joint sponsorship of the National Tsing Hua University Research Fellowship Fund and the China Institute in America. New York: The Institute, 1954. Pp. 68.

295. *Ten Years of Educational Exchange: The Fulbright Program in Japan 1951-1961.* Tokyo: United States Educational Commission in Japan, 1961.

296. Tryon, Ruth W. *Investment in Creative Scholarship: A History of the Fellowship Program of the American Association of University Women 1890-1956.* Washington, D.C.: The Association, 1957.

297. <u>Twenty Years of United States Government Programs in Cultural Relations</u>. Rev. ed. New York: Committee on Educational Interchange Policy, Institute of International Education, 1959. Pp. 30.

   A brief history of the ideas, institutions, and legislation which have shaped United States cultural relations policies. The report defends three conclusions: (a) United States government activity in international cultural relations is based on sound principles of objectivity, reciprocity, and wide private citizen participation; (b) the programs have had favorable results in the United States and abroad, and (c) the programs are growing and evolving.

298. Young, Francis A. "The Conference Board of Associated Research Councils in the United States: A Brief Historical Account with Special Reference to National and International Manpower Problems." (See No. 714.)

CHAPTER 8 RESEARCH ON EDUCATIONAL EXCHANGE

299. Bennett, John W. "Cross-Cultural Education Research and the Study of National Acculturation" in Some Uses of Anthropology: Theoretical and Applied. Ed. Joseph B. Casagrande and Thomas Gladwin. Washington, D.C.: Anthropological Society of Washington, 1956, pp. 1-22.

*300. Cormack, Margaret L. An Evaluation of Research on Educational Exchange. Prepared for the Bureau of Educational and Cultural Affairs, United States Department of State. New York: Brooklyn College, 1962. Pp. 137.

With the goal of summarizing and evaluating research on educational exchange, the author scrutinizes the more sophisticated methodologies and trends in research and assesses their conclusions. Included are bibliographies of dissertations, studies sponsored by the United States Department of State, and a general bibliograpny on educational exchange.

301. Cussler, Margaret. Review of Selected Studies Affecting International Educational and Cultural Affairs. Prepared for the United States Advisory Commission on International Educational and Cultural Affairs as part of a larger study on the effectiveness of the United States Department of State Cultural Exchange Program. Washington, D.C.: Bureau of Educational and Cultural Affairs, United States Department of State, 1962. Pp. 94.

302. Du Bois, Cora. "Research in Cross-Cultural Education," Institute of International Education: News Bulletin, XXVIII (June, 1953), 5-8, 60-64.

303. Herman, Simon N., and Schild, Erling O. "Contexts for the Study of Cross-Cultural Education," <u>Journal of Social Psychology</u>, LII (November, 1960), 231-50.

304. Jacobsen, Joseph M. <u>A Study of Three Related Research Projects</u>. ("NAFSA Studies and Papers Research Series," No. 3.) New York: National Association for Foreign Student Affairs, 1962. Pp. 17.

Describes in detail the findings of three research programs: (a) research conducted by the Institute of Research on Overseas Programs at Michigan State University, (b) International Cooperation Administration research on its participant training programs, and (c) research on the effects of nine foreign-student orientation programs by Stuart W. Cook, Joan Havel, and June R. Christ.

305. Jacobson, Eugene H., Kumata, Hideya, and Gullahorn, Jeanne E. "Cross-Cultural Contributions to Attitude Research," <u>Public Opinion Quarterly</u>, XXIV (Summer, 1960), 205-23.

306. Klineberg, Otto. "Research on International Exchanges in Education, Science, and Culture." Typescript. Prepared for an International Social Science Council meeting on the above topic, April 8-10, 1964, in Tel Aviv.

An excellent presentation of findings gleaned from available research with helpful pointers toward future investigations. A discussion of study abroad touches upon the following: (a) personal contacts and interpersonal relations, (b) the impact of academic success or failure, (c) the sojourn experience and the U-curve phenomenon, (d) the problem of immigration, (e) racial and ethnic aspects, (f) effects of exchange on the host country, and (g) the desirable age or level of education of exchangees. Personal contacts involved in technical cooperation and the problems of personnel selection and training are also treated. A bibliography is included.

*307. Mestenhauser, Josef A. (ed.). <u>Research in Programs for Foreign Students: A Report of the Waldenwoods Seminar</u>. ("NAFSA Studies and Papers Research Series," No. 2.) New York: National Association for Foreign Student Affairs, 1961.

A major contribution to the task of describing and evaluating the growing literature. Leading social scientists, specialists in higher education, and a representative group of foreign student advisers from several colleges and universities met to examine recent research. General session reports discuss how to apply research and suggest implications for the future of foreign students in American higher education. Seven committee reports are also included: (a) admissions, selection, and pre-departure planning; (b) reception, orientation, and housing; (c) academic achievement and counseling; (d) English language; (e) extracurricular activities of foreign students in the United States; (f) counseling the foreign student, and (g) terminal experience, departure, and follow-up.

*308. Porter, Robert D. (ed.). Selected Studies in Intercultural Education. ("NAFSA Studies and Papers Research Series," No. 4.) New York: National Association for Foreign Student Affairs, 1962. Pp. 16.

Detailed reviews of twenty-two studies arranged under the headings of national studies, effects of study abroad, problem areas, and personality concepts.

309. Research in International Education. New York: National Association for Foreign Student Affairs and the Institute of International Education, annually.

Information on the purpose, scope, method, and major findings of research in progress and recently completed.

310. Smith, M. Brewster. "A Program of Research on Student Exchange," Institute of International Education: News Bulletin, XXIX (May, 1954), 2-6.

311. _____. "Report on the Work of the Committee on Cross-Cultural Education," Items (Social Science Research Council), XII (December, 1958), 40-42.

312. _____. "Research in the Field of International Education" in *Handbook on International Study*. New York: Institute of International Education, 1955, pp. 235-52.

*313. Warmbrunn, Werner (ed.). *Research Studies in Intercultural Education: Reviews and Implications for Exchange of Persons*. ("NAFSA Studies and Papers Research Series," No. 1.) New York: National Association for Foreign Student Affairs, 1960. Pp. 18.

Reviews of studies coupled with suggestions for improvement of exchange programs. Ten lengthy studies are discussed: *The Foreign Student in the New York Area*, George A. Beebe; *The Foreign Student in American Colleges*, Edward C. Cieslak; *Foreign Students and Higher Education in the United States*, Cora Du Bois; *Exchange of Persons: The Evolution of Cross-Cultural Education*, Guy S. Metraux; *Cultural Attitudes and International Understanding*, Hilda Taba; *No Frontier to Learning: The Mexican Student in the United States*, Ralph L. Beals and Norman D. Humphrey; *Indian Students on an American Campus*, Richard D. Lambert and Marvin Bressler; *The American Experience of Swedish Students: Retrospect and Aftermath*, Franklin D. Scott; *The Western-Educated Man in India: A Study of His Role and Influence*, John and Ruth H. Useem; *Learning Across Cultures: A Study of Germans Visiting America*, Jeanne Watson and Ronald Lippitt.

PART IV

EDUCATIONAL EXCHANGE:
UNITED STATES NATIONALS ABROAD

CHAPTER **9** UNITED STATES STUDENTS ABROAD

PHILOSOPHY, CURRICULA, AND ORGANIZATION

This section and the one which follows inevitably overlap; however, a useful distinction can be made between those studies that are more policy-oriented and those that are designed for the generation of social-psychological theory on attitude change and adjustment in a foreign culture.

314. Abrams, Irwin. "Overseas Travel-Study Programs in U.S. Higher Education," <u>Goals for Higher Education in a Decade of Decision: Current Issues in Higher Education, 1961</u>. Ed. G. Kerry Smith. Proceedings, 16th Annual National Conference on Higher Education, Association of Higher Education, 1961, pp. 220-23.

Three basic questions are addressed to foreign study planners: "(a) How profound is the cultural immersion in the foreign community? (b) What is the academic content of the program abroad? and (c) How is the program related to the student's entire education?"

315. _____. "Preface to Study Abroad," <u>Journal of General Education</u>, XIV (January, 1963), 220-29.

316. _____. "The Student Abroad" in <u>Higher Education: Some Newer Developments</u>. Ed. Samuel Baskin. New York: McGraw-Hill Book Co., Inc., 1965, pp. 78-103.

317. _____. <u>Study Abroad</u>. ("New Dimensions in Higher Education," No. 6, OE-50014.) Washington, D.C.: Office of Education, United States Department of Health, Education and Welfare, 1960. Pp. 21.

The author discusses the development and objectives of the study-abroad programs, common program patterns, how to test program quality, and problems and prospects.

318. *Academic Programs Abroad: An Exploration of Their Assets and Liabilities.* New York: Institute of International Education, 1960. Pp. 30.

    This summary of a conference at Mount Holyoke College discusses guidance, information services, educational facilities in non-European areas, language problems, and evaluation.

319. *American Students Abroad: Goodwill Ambassadors?* Syracuse, N.Y.: Maxwell Graduate School of Citizenship and Public Affairs, Syracuse University, 1958.

320. Battsek, M. "A Practical Analysis of Some Aspects of Study Abroad," *Journal of General Education*, XIII (January, 1962), 225-42.

321. Ezell, Stiles D. "Foreign Medical Education for United States Students," *Institute for International Education: News Bulletin*, XXXIII (October, 1957), 13-17.

322. Freed, Marjorie. "Antioch Education Abroad," *Institute of International Education: News Bulletin*, XXXVI (January, 1961), 19-25.

    The Antioch program tries to develop a combination of study, work, travel, and life abroad. During a college year 100 of 1,200 students are studying or working in one of 15 foreign countries. This arrangement allows Antioch to expand its total enrollment by about 8 per cent. The students attend the same classes as nationals and live with local families.

323. Freeman, Stephen A. "International Study at Home and Abroad" in "The Non-Western World in Higher Education." (See No. 95.)

324. _____. "National Conference on Undergraduate Study Abroad," *Liberal Education*, XLVII (March, 1961), 23-31.

*325. _____. *Undergraduate Study Abroad.* Report of Consultative Service on United States

Undergraduate Study Abroad. New York: Institute of International Education, 1964. Pp. 126.

An excellent analysis of various aspects of undergraduate study-abroad programs. The author warns that

> . . . the intentions have generally been good and the motives praiseworthy. However, the failure of some colleges to examine their objectives and evaluate the results critically and realistically, the lack of adequate information about the foreign scene and especially the foreign educational systems, the pressure of student demand and sometimes of faculty demand, the duplication of effort, the shoddiness of some attempts, and many other reasons are now creating a situation which in some aspects threatens to become a national educational scandal.

Included are directories of academic year and summer study-abroad programs and a bibliography.

326. Garraty, John Arthur, and Adams, Walter. From Main Street to the Left Bank; Students and Scholars Abroad. East Lansing: Michigan State University Press, 1959. Pp. 216.

In a "plain talk" discussion, the authors point out the advantages and liabilities of college and university programs of education in Europe. Their impressions touch on broad administrative, academic, and personal aspects. An appendix provides a description of several programs of American colleges.

327. Gould, Samuel B. "The University's Stake in Educational Travel" in The American Student Abroad 1956-57. New York: Council on Student Travel, 1958, pp. 5-7.

328. Guggenheim, Michael. "Sur le Pont D'Avignon avec Bryn Mawr," Overseas, II (March, 1963), 21-23.

329. Gullahorn, John T. and Jeanne E. "American Ojectives in Study Abroad; A Study Conducted

by Interview and Questionnaire," <u>Journal of Higher Education</u>, XXIX (October, 1958), 369-74.

330. Hagberg, Peter. "An American Student in Africa," <u>Overseas</u>, III (October, 1963), 18-22.

331. Haskins, Lewis M. "The Foreign Study Program at Earlham College," <u>Journal of General Education</u>, XIII (January, 1962), 262-67.

332. Kaufmann, Fritz. "Academic Travel Abroad," <u>Institute of International Education: News Bulletin</u>, XXXVI (March, 1961), 25-29.

333. Kehoe, Monika. "Higher Education in Ethiopia," <u>Journal of Higher Education</u>, XXXIII (December, 1962), 475-78.

After the author briefly describes the main problems of the Haile Selassie University (unqualified students and a European-type education poorly suited to Ethiopian needs), she suggests that the United States government bring fewer African students to the United States and send more American students to Ethiopia under something like a junior-year-abroad plan. The benefit to the American student is obvious; meanwhile the American student provides an example to the Africans that is unlike the stereotype. Benefit will also accrue to the Africans through encouragement to speak English outside of class.

334. Klein, Roger H. (ed.). <u>Young Americans Abroad</u>. New York: Harper & Row, 1963. Pp. 270.

First-hand reports by ten young Americans who lived and worked abroad.

335. Matthew, R. J. "Sweet Briar's Junior Year in France," <u>College and University</u>, XXXVI (Spring, 1961), 330-37.

336. Pace, Charles R. <u>The Junior Year in France: An Evaluation of the University of Delaware-- Sweet Briar College Program</u>. Syracuse, N.Y.: Published for Sweet Briar College by Syracuse University Press, 1959. Pp. 69.

337. Randall, Helen W. "Smith's Junior Year Abroad," <u>Institute of International Education:</u>

News Bulletin, XXXVI (February, 1961), 13-19.

The American and European educational systems are difficult to mix--general and democratic versus specialized and intellectually exclusive. Therefore, the student in the junior year abroad finds adjustment extremely difficult. Smith hires local professors in Paris, Madrid, and Florence to give American-style courses in their own languages.

*338. Shank, Donald J. "The Junior Year Abroad: A A Critical Look," Institute of International Education: News Bulletin, XXXVI (October, 1960), 11-19.

The author offers several generalizations: (a) Most United States undergraduates are not "really" in foreign universities because they take special courses in English which are less difficult. (b) All students say the junior year abroad is the richest experience of their lives. (c) Students feel the experience is in the realm of general education rather than in their major field. (d) All students achieve a language competence they would not achieve at home. (e) Intimate relations with nationals depend on living quarters. (f) Students often criticize the United States leaders in charge of the programs who often do not know the university well enough. (g) Overcrowding in foreign European universities is occurring. (h) Better planning is needed in all programs.

339. _____. "Programs for American Students Abroad: A Critique," National Association of Women Deans and Counselors: Journal, XXVII (Winter, 1964), 74-76.

340. _____, et al. "Opportunities and Problems Involved in the Study Abroad of United States Students; Panel Discussion," College and University, XXXVIII (Summer, 1963), 434-60.

This panel discussion covers these aspects of the general topic: the Fulbright program, present and future programs of universities and colleges, practical problems of sending students overseas, and problems of developing the new programs.

341. "Study Abroad: Trends, Problems, Recommendations; Panel Discussion," *College and University*, XL (Summer, 1965), 434-36.

342. Taba, Hilda. *Cultural Attitudes and International Understanding: An Evaluation of an International Study Tour*. ("Occasional Paper," No. 5.) New York: Institute of International Education, 1953.

343. *Transplanted Students*. A Report summarizing the discussions and recommendations of the National Conference on Undergraduate Study Abroad. New York: Institute of International Education, 1961. Pp. 19.

    Subjects discussed are goals of education, overcrowding, selection of students, scholarship aid, and credit evaluation.

344. Wallace, John A. "Characteristics of Programs for Study Abroad," *Journal of General Education*, XIII (January, 1962), 251-61. University Park: Pennsylvania State University Press, 1962. Reprinted.

345. Watson, Curtis B. "A Fraternity of Understanding," *Overseas*, II (April, 1963), 10-13.

346. Weaver, Paul. "Study Abroad and General Education," *Journal of General Education*, XIII (January, 1962), 243-50.

347. Weidner, Edward W. and Jean B. "American University Women Abroad," *Institute of International Education: News Bulletin*, XXXIV (November, 1958), 24-28.

ATTITUDES AND ADJUSTMENT

348. Gullahorn, John T. and Jeanne E. *American Students in France*. Lawrence: University of Kansas, 1956. Pp. 244.

349. Herman, Simon N. "American Jewish Students in Israel: A Social Psychological Study in Cross-Cultural Education," *Jewish Social Studies*, XXIV (January, 1962), 3-29.

350. _____, and Schild, Erling O. "Ethnic Role Conflict in a Cross-Cultural Situation," Human Relations, XIII (August, 1960), 215-28.

351. _____, and _____. "The Stranger-Group in a Cross-Cultural Situation," Sociometry, XXIV (June, 1961), 165-76.

352. Leonard, Elizabeth W. "Attitude Change in a College Program of Foreign Study and Travel," Educational Record, XLV (Winter, 1964), 173-81.

Recent studies show that attitudes prior to experience in a foreign culture will generally determine the attitudes one will have upon return. The author uses information from a study of a student-abroad program at Adelphi University and asks whether significant attitude changes did develop. The results indicate that foreign study and travel induce a greater attitude change and in a shorter time than a normal program of campus study. Specific changes related to the following variables are discussed: age, religion, sex, intelligence, socio-economic status, and country of study. A bibliography is included.

353. McGuigan, F. J. "Psychological Changes Related to Intercultural Experiences," Psychological Reports, IV (March, 1958), 55-60.

CHAPTER **10** UNITED STATES TEACHERS AND SCHOLARS ABROAD

354. Bureau of Social Science Research, Inc. <u>Cross-Cultural Education and Its Impact</u>. 2 vols. Washington, D.C.: Bureau of Educational and Cultural Affairs, United States Department of State.

    Part I. <u>A Survey of American Recipients of U.S. Educational Exchange Awards Under Public Law 584</u>. 1953. Pp. 34.

    Part II. <u>A Survey of American Recipients of U.S. Government Awards Entailing Affiliation with Academic Institutions Abroad and Excluding Public Law 584 Grants</u>. 1954. Pp. 18.

355. Goodwin, Leonard. <u>American Professors in Asia: A Study of the Selection and Adaptation of Fifty American Professors Who Went to India, Pakistan, and Korea Under the Fulbright-Hays Program During 1962-63</u>. Washington, D.C.: Prepared for the Bureau of Educational and Cultural Affairs, United States Department of State, 1964. Pp. 83.

The author hopes to develop methods to improve the selection of Fulbright professors going to less-developed countries and also to help develop a theory of cross-cultural adaptation. Predictions of overseas effectiveness were based on personal interviews and other information. Predictions were later correlated with assessments of actual effectiveness.

356. Griffin, W. H. "American Educators Abroad," <u>Journal of Teacher Education</u>, XI (March, 1960), 33-39.

357. Gullahorn, John T. and Jeanne E. "American Fulbrighters Back Home," *Institute of International Education: News Bulletin*, XXXIV (April, 1959), 13-19.

358. _____, and _____. *International Educational Exchange: An Assessment of Professional and Social Contributions by American Fulbright and Smith-Mundt Grantees: 1947-1957*. 5 vols. Report prepared for the Program Evaluation Staff of the International Educational Exchange Service, United States Department of State. East Lansing: Michigan State University, 1960.

359. _____, and _____. *Professional and Social Consequences of Fulbright and Smith-Mundt Awards*. Washington, D.C.: International Educational Exchange Service, United States Department of State, 1958.

360. _____, and _____. "The Role of the Academic Man as a Cross-Cultural Mediator," *American Sociological Review*, XXV (June, 1960), 414-17.

361. _____, and _____. "Visiting Fulbright Professors as Agents of Cross-Cultural Communication," *Sociology and Social Research*, XLVI (April, 1962), 282-93.

362. Macgregor, Gordon. *The Experiences of American Scholars in Countries of the Near East and South Asia*. Report submitted by the Advisory Committee for the Near East and South Asia to the Committee on International Exchange of Persons, Conference Board of Associated Research Councils. Washington, D.C.: The Board, 1957. Pp. 96.

Report on the problems of selection, planning, and personal adjustment of Americans in the Fulbright programs with Egypt, India, and Iraq.

363. Mendelsohn, Harold, and Orenstein, Frank E. "A Survey of Fulbright Award Recipients: Cross-Cultural Education and Its Impacts," *Public Opinion Quarterly*, XIX (Winter, 1955-56), 401-7.

PART V

EDUCATIONAL EXCHANGE: FOREIGN
NATIONALS IN THE UNITED STATES

CHAPTER **11** FOREIGN STUDENTS

PHILOSOPHY, CURRICULA, AND ORGANIZATION

This section and the next inevitably overlap; nevertheless it seems useful to distinguish between works that deal explicitly with policy and program organization and those works that report the attitudes and adjustment problems of foreign students. The latter studies are often oriented toward the generation of social-psychological theory on attitude change and adjustment in a foreign culture. For practical suggestions culled from the theoretical literature, see Chapter 8 and the publications of the National Association for Foreign Student Affairs in particular.

364. Abrams, Freda and Irwin. "A Different Kind of Discipline," Overseas, II (May, 1963), 17-22.

   The Antioch work-study program for foreign students.

365. Adams, Don. "Cultural Pitfalls of a Foreign Educational Adviser," Peabody Journal of Education, XXXVI (May, 1959), 338-44.

366. African Students in the United States: A Guide for Sponsors of Student Exchange Programs with Africa. New York: Committee on Educational Interchange Policy, Institute of International Education, 1960. Pp. 30.

   This pamphlet offers such pertinent contemporary and background information as (a) countries the students come from, (b) their sponsors, (c) what they study and on what academic level, and (d) pros and cons of Africans studying at segregated institutions. The report concludes with a list of questions which United States colleges and universities should ask themselves when deciding policy. Statistical information and a bibliography are also provided.

367. Awasthi, S. P. "An Experiment in Voluntary Repatriation of High-Level Technical Manpower--The Scientists' Pool," The Economic Weekly (Bombay), XVII (September 18, 1965), 1,447-52. Excerpts reprinted in Development Digest, IV (April, 1966), 28-35.

368. Bang, Katherine C. "The Foreign Student Adviser and Community Resources," Part VII of Handbook for Foreign Student Advisers. New York: National Association of Foreign Student Advisers (now National Association for Foreign Student Affairs), 1959.

369. Beal, Harriet (ed.). Guide for Campus International Programs. Washington, D.C.: United States National Student Association, 1965. Pp. 56.

370. Beck, Robert H. "The Professional Training in Education of Foreign Students in the United States," Journal of Teacher Education, XIII, Part I (June, 1962), 140-49; Part II (September, 1962), 302-18; Parts III and IV (December, 1962), 402-8.

371. Beebe, George A. The Foreign Student in the New York City Area. A Final Report of One Year of Study. New York: Greater New York Council for Foreign Students, 1955. Pp. 144. (Out of print.)

A bibliography is included.

372. Berbusse, Edward J. "The Foreign Student on the American Catholic Campus," Liberal Education, XLV (October, 1959), 428-37.

373. Berg, Sherwood O. "University Training in Agricultural Economics for Foreign Students," Journal of Farm Economics, XLI (December, 1959), 1373-83.

374. Broadhurst, Martha Jean. Nurses from Abroad: Values in International Exchange of Persons.

New York: The American Nurses Foundation, 1962. Pp. 144.

375. Cajoleas, Louis P. "Counseling Overseas Students," *Journal of Higher Education*, XXIX (April, 1958), 209-12.

The counselor must understand his own culture and the former environment of the foreign student. The counseling may be active (create opportunities to solve problems through meaningful experience) or passive (make services available to the student which he may use on his own initiative). The counselor must also help the student become aware of the problems of readjusting to home values and changes.

376. Cieslak, Edward C. *The Foreign Student in American Colleges: A Survey and Evaluation of Administrative Problems and Practices.* Detroit: Wayne State University Press, 1955. Pp. 175.

Originally a thesis submitted to Wayne State University. A bibliography is included.

*377. *The College, the University and the Foreign Student.* New York: Committee on the Foreign Student in American Colleges and Universities, National Association for Foreign Student Affairs, 1963.

The first part of this brief pamphlet discusses the interest of the university, the nation, and the international community in educational exchange. The second part inquires into the responsibilities of the university to the foreign student with regard to policies on admission, English language, orientation, academic advising, personal counseling, and the foreign student as an alumnus. This "Langmuir Report" urges constitutional definition of goals, frequent assessment of accomplishments, and high administrative support for international exchange efforts.

378. *Conference Report.* New York: National Association for Foreign Student Affairs, annually.

Includes addresses and discussion proceedings on a wide variety of topics involving American universities and foreign students.

379. Cook, Stuart W., Christ, June R., and Havel, Joan. "The Effects of an Orientation Program for Foreign Students." 10 vol. Mimeo., Research Center for Human Relations, New York University, 1955.

380. Coombs, Philip A. "International Educational Exchange: A Work for Many Hands," Higher Education, XVIII (September, 1961), 3-6.

381. _____. "A 10-Point Agenda," Overseas, I (February, 1962), 2-5.

382. Cormack, Margaret L. "Three Steps to Better Orientation: 'Cultural Shock' Can Be Warded Off," Overseas, III (September, 1963), 11-15.

383. Counseling Foreign Students. ("Studies Series," No. 6; "Student Personnel Work," No. 15, XIV.) Washington, D.C.: The American Council on Education, 1950. Pp. 54.

384. Darrah, L. B. "Preparing Foreign Students to Study Farm Economic Problems in Their Own Countries," Journal of Farm Economics, XLI (December, 1959), 1,384-92.

385. Davis, James M. "Is Too Much Being Done for the Foreign Student?" Institute of International Education: News Bulletin, XXXIII (November, 1957), 6-12.

386. _____. "The Most Effective and Helpful Means of Educating and Dealing with the Increasing Number of Foreign Students Attending American Colleges and Universities," Goals for Higher Education in a Decade of Decisions: Current Issues in Higher Education, 1961. Ed. G. Kerry Smith. Proceedings, 16th National Conference on Higher Education, Association for Higher Education, 1961, pp. 101-4.

*387. _____. "Some Trends in International Educational Exchange," Comparative Education Review, VIII (June, 1964), 48-57.

In this article the author discusses in depth five projections based on recent developments.

(1) International educational exchange will increase. (2) The purpose of the agencies and individuals involved will be clarified. (3) Procedures at all levels will be improved. (4) Research into all aspects of cross-cultural relations will be continued and expanded. (5) Individuals involved in the operations of these programs will grow in competence and understanding: there will be an increasing professionalization of personnel.

388. DuBois, Cora. *Foreign Students and Higher Education in the United States.* Prepared for the Carnegie Endowment for International Peace and the Institute of International Education. Washington, D.C.: American Council on Education, 1956. Pp. 221.

The author views the foreign student from the perspective of (a) the administrative agencies involved, (b) the concerns of the researcher, and (c) the problems of orientating the student to the host environment.

389. *Educational Exchange in the Economic Development of Nations.* New York: Committee on Educational Interchange Policy, Institute of International Education, 1961. Pp. 25.

390. *Expanding University Enrollment and the Foreign Student; A Case for Foreign Students at U.S. Colleges and Universities.* New York: Committee on Educational Interchange Policy, Institute of International Education, 1957. Pp. 10.

391. Feraru, Arthur. *Survey of How Foreign Students Learned of the Educational Institution Where They Are Now Enrolled.* New York: Institute of International Education, 1962.

*392. *Foreign Professors and Research Scholars at U.S. Colleges and Universities.* New York: Committee on Educational Interchange Policy, Institute of International Education, 1963.

An admirable analysis of a little-explored topic. Foreign professors and research scholars come to the United States because (a) the academic world is becoming more mobile and communication across national boundaries is increasing, (b) United States institutions are experiencing greater prestige, (c) research facilities are especially attractive, (d) a shortage of staff members at United States colleges and universities has stimulated overseas recruitment, (e) the drive for modernization in less-developed countries and United States participation in this process brings more scholars to the United States, (f) economic inducements are attractive, and (g) academic environments in home countries are occasionally unattractive. The most important single conclusion of the study is that colleges and universities are not making full use of foreign scholars as an educational resource. An extensive statistical appendix is included.

393. The Foreign Student, Exchangee or Immigrant? New York: Committee on Educational Interchange Policy, Institute of International Education, 1958. Pp. 17.

A discussion of the foreign student who takes up permanent residence in the United States.

394. A Foreign Student Program for the Developing Countries During the Coming Decade. New York: Committee on Educational Interchange Policy, Institute of International Education, 1962.

The thesis of this pamphlet is that a proper foreign student program for the developing countries can be evolved by ". . . the educational community, in cooperation with the United States and foreign governments . . . without resorting to central direction."

395. Fox, Melvin J. "Foreign Students in American Colleges." ("Ford Foundation Reprint.") New York: Office of Reports, Ford Foundation, 1962. Pp. 8.

Although foreign students are found in 1,666 institutions, only 150 of them have more than 50 foreign students. The latter group of universities and colleges must especially reassess present programs. The author suggests that transitional programs be offered to foreign students unable to meet present qualifications and that training be more directly related to national development plans.

396. Gillett, Margaret. "Orientation of Foreign Students in the United States," Overseas Education, XXXIII,4 (January, 1962), 171-75.

397. The Goals of Student Exchange. New York: Committee on Educational Interchange Policy, Institute of International Education, 1955. Pp. 15.

398. Goldstein, Marcia Gray. The Indian Student: A Survey of His Background, Educational Aspirations, and Perceived Vocational Opportunities. ("International Student Studies Series," No. 9.) Lawrence: University of Kansas, 1964.

399. Gullahorn, John T. and Jeanne E. Foreign Student Leaders on American Campuses: An Experiment in Cross-Cultural Education. A Partial Evaluation. Prepared for the Foreign Student Leadership Project of the United States National Student Association. Lawrence: University of Kansas, 1958. Pp. 131.

400. Halberstam, Jacob L., and Dacso, Michael. "Foreign and United States Residents in University-Affiliated Teaching Hospitals: An Investigation of United States Graduate Medical Education," Bulletin of the New York Academy of Medicine, LXII (March, 1966), 182-208.

401. Haniotis, George V. "An Exercise in Voluntary Repatriation in Greece," The OECD Observer (Paris), 11 (August, 1964), 12-15. Excerpts reprinted in Development Digest, IV (April, 1966), 36-41.

*402. Harari, Maurice. "American Higher Education and the Foreign Student: Laissez-Faire Versus Planning." A speech delivered at the Annual Conference of the National Association for

Foreign Student Affairs, Philadelphia, April 29, 1965. Mimeo., The Association, New York, 1965. Pp. 10.

"Intelligent planning sets the framework or foundation for fruitful freedom or laissez-faire. Without good planning we have . . . not freedom, but wasteful and heartbreaking chaos." Among several suggestions for improved planning is one calling for a "network of multi-purpose field offices overseas" to inform and coordinate operations of agencies and colleges and universities.

403. Henderson, Gregory. "Foreign Students: Exchange or Immigration? An American Looks at a 'Near-Scandalous' Situation," International Development Review, VI (December, 1964), 19-21.

404. Henry, David D. "The 1960 Nigerian-American Scholarship Program," Institute of International Education: News Bulletin, XXXVI (November, 1960), 17-25.

The author describes joint action by a group of American colleges in cooperation with the Nigerian government to finance four years of undergraduate education for African students.

*405. Higbee, Homer D. The Status of Foreign-Student Advising in United States Universities and Colleges. East Lansing: Institute of Research on Overseas Programs, Michigan State University, 1961. Pp. 62.

The author writes:

> In addition to surveying the range and scope of services provided to international students, this study presents a profile of the people primarily responsible for these services, and attempts to determine the educational and/or other objectives underlying the allocation of resources to international educational activities of which the foreign student program is one major element.

Extensive statistical information is offered. The author concludes with several specific recommendations for improvement of foreign-student advisory programs.

406. Huerta, Czarina. *African Student Exchange and Service Programs*. Chicago: National Catholic Conference for Interracial Justice, 1961. Pp. 52. (Out of print.) "A Summary of *African Student Exchange and Service Programs*." Mimeo., The Conference, 1961. Pp. 5.

407. Kincaid, Harry V. *A Study of a Sample of Foreign Students in the United States*. 2 vols. (Stanford Research Institute Project No. IM-3616.) Washington, D.C.: Bureau of Educational and Cultural Affairs, United States Department of State, December, 1961.

408. King, John A., Jr. "The Student from Abroad at the Harvard Law School," *Institute of International Education: News Bulletin*, XXXIII (October, 1957), 18-23.

409. Kitchen, Robert W., Jr. "A Continuing Obligation," *College and University*, XL (Summer, 1965), 396-401.

410. *Land-Grant Centennial Lectures and Students from Abroad, 1961-1962*. Washington, D.C.: National Association of State Universities and Land-Grant Colleges, 1963.

411. Leuallen, Dean E. Emerson. "Individual Programs for Foreign Pharmacists: Columbia Pharmacy's Unique System," *Overseas*, III (September, 1963), 3-7.

412. Lippitt, Ronald, and Watson, Jeanne. "Some Special Problems of Learning and the Teaching Process in Cross-Cultural Education," *International Social Science Bulletin*, VII,1 (1955), 59-65.

Title of *Bulletin* changed to *Journal* in 1959.

413. Lorenz, Reuben. "Problems of Cost and Programming of Foreign Visitors on the American Campus." Mimeo., American Council on Education, 1961.

414. McCullough, Mabelle G., and Mestenhauser, Josef A. "Housing of Foreign Students--An

Educational Experience?," <u>Journal of College Personnel</u>, V (October, 1963), 2-7.

The authors discuss the relationship of the housing situation to the attainment of English-language proficiency and international-exchange goals in general.

415. <u>Military Assistance Training Programs of the U.S. Government</u>. New York: Committee on Educational Interchange Policy, Institute of International Education, 1964.

416. Morgan, Gordon D. "Exploratory Study of Problems of Academic Adjustment of Nigerian Students in America," <u>Journal of Negro Education</u>, XXXII (Summer, 1963), 208-17.

417. Moulton, W. N. "Science, Education, and Students from the Underdeveloped Nations," <u>Science Education</u>, XLIX (April, 1965), 220-25.

418. Murase, Kenneth. "International Students in Education for Social Work: An Assessment by International Graduates of Schools of Social Work in North America, 1948-57," <u>Social Service Review</u>, XXXV (June, 1961), 171-83.

419. Murphy, E. J. "African Exchange Problems," <u>Institute of International Education: News Bulletin</u>, XXXVI (November, 1960), 11-16.

The following are among the many insights: (a) Programs must be organized with an explicit purpose in mind and should fit the government's needs. (b) Clear and respectable standards of selection are needed to obtain the best qualified students and to protect the image of United States quality education. (c) The granting of partial scholarships should be avoided.

420. Neal, Joe W. "Developing the International Office," <u>Overseas</u>, III (April, 1964), 7-11.

421. Nelson, Robert L. "The Psychiatric Needs of Foreign Students," <u>Institute of International Education: News Bulletin</u>, XXXIII (May, 1958), 13-17.

422. _____. "The Use of Psychiatric Facilities in a University by Foreign Students" in The Student and Mental Health, an International View. Ed. D. L. Funkenstein. New York: World Federation for Mental Health, 1959.

423. Neumeyer, Martin H. and Peterson, James A. "Problems of Foreign Students," Sociology and Social Research, XXXII (March-April, 1948), 787-92.

424. Olsen, Erling. "Why Do Foreign Scholars Want to Stay in the U.S.?," ACLS Newsletter, XV (November, 1964), 8-10.

425. Orientation of Foreign Students: Signposts for the Cultural Maze. New York: Committee on Educational Interchange Policy, Institute of International Education, 1956. Pp. 18.

426. Otis, Jack. "Psychotherapy with Foreign Students in a University," Mental Hygiene, XXXIX (October, 1955), 581-97.

427. Parsons, Kenneth H., and Kaihara, Motosuke. "A Note: Graduate Training of Foreign Students in Agricultural Economics," Journal of Farm Economics, XLI (February, 1959), 128-32.

428. Platt, Joseph B. "Emigration of Scholars and the Development of Taiwan: Chinese-American Cooperation," Development Digest, IV (April, 1966), 42-46.

The article consists of excerpts from a paper presented to the panel on science policy for development at the Seventh World Conference of the Society for International Development, Washington, D.C., March 12, 1965.

429. Pratt, Dallas. "Helping the Foreign Student in New York City: An Experiment in Brief Psychotherapy and Cultural Research," Bulletin of the World Federation for Mental Health, IV (November, 1952), 172-76.

430. Pritchard, Edith M. "Hospital Programs for Foreign Nurses," Institute of International Education: News Bulletin, XXXIV (May, 1959), 29-35.

431. Raushenbush, Esther. The Fulbright Professor Meets the American College. New York: John Hay Whitney Foundation, 1962. Pp. 59.

432. Ruedisili, Chester H. "Foreign Students Surveyed at University of Wisconsin," Overseas, III (April, 1964), 18-22.

433. Sanders, Irwin T. The Professional Education of Students from Other Lands. New York: Council on Social Work Education, 1963.

434. Sayre, Joan M. "A Report of Speech and Language Programs Available to Foreign Students in the U.S. at Institutions of Higher Education," Asha, VI (May, 1964), 155-56.

435. Schmidt, J. P. "Discussion: Postgraduate Instruction for Foreign Students," Journal of Farm Economics, XLI (December, 1959), 1, 395-97.

436. Shank, Donald J. "Student Exchanges," Educational Record, XXXVII (April, 1956), 111-14.

437. Sloan, Ruth C., and Cummings, Ivor G. A Survey of African Students Studying in the United States. New York: Phelps-Stokes Fund, 1949. Pp. 78.

438. Smythe, H. H. and M. M. "African Student Selection Programs," Institute of International Education: News Bulletin, XXXVI (November, 1960), 34-40.

The author pleads for more coordination in selecting African students because individual, church, civic, social, state, and many other organizations are using inferior standards of selection. Coordination for these programs could be obtained through a central screening agency that would be able to develop testing, interviewing, and other techniques for application at several regional centers on the continent.

439. Stearns, Troy L. "Discussion: Post Graduate Instruction for Foreign Students," Journal of Farm Economics, XLI (December, 1959), 1, 392-95.

FOREIGN STUDENTS 93

*440. Storm, William B., and Gable, Richard W. "Foreign Students in the United States: The Problem of Achieving Maximum Benefits," <u>Educational Record</u>, XLII (October, 1961), 304-15.

The authors focus on the question of how foreign students at the University of Southern California benefit from their experience and explain in detail five critical factors in making the foreign students' education productive and successful: (a) careful selection, (b) predeparture and postarrival orientation, including American pedagogical techniques, (c) assurance that the student studies something that will be useful upon his return home, (d) development of a fundamental understanding of our culture without alienation from his own, (e) availability of follow-up help after return home. A bibliography is included.

441. Strain, William H. "Problems of Educational Exchange with English-Speaking Countries of West and East Africa," <u>College and University</u>, XLI (Winter, 1966), 145-61.

*442. _____, et al. "Post-Admission Adjustment Problems of Foreign Students: A Panel Discussion," <u>College and University</u>, XXXVII (Summer, 1962), 414-43.

The topics and panelists include "New Directions in the Foreign Student Program," Donald J. Shank; "Plan for United States Government Action Respecting Foreign Students in the United States," Marita Houlihan; "Academic Needs of Foreign Students: Some Unresolved Dilemmas Facing American Higher Education," Homer D. Higbee; "The Post-Admission Adjustment of Foreign Students," Robert D. Porter.

443. <u>Student Government and Foreign Student Programming</u>. Washington, D.C.: United States National Student Association, 1962.

444. Tanenhaus, Joseph, and Roth, Sidney G. "Non-Immigrant Foreign Students: A Survey of Their Needs and Interests," <u>Journal of Experimental Education</u>, XXXI (December, 1962), 173-76.

A survey of 384 foreign students at New York

University used a questionnaire designed to help the university better its facilities for these students. Included is a description of the methodology of the study, a list of the needs and difficulties of foreign students, and a summary and recommendations.

445. Thurston, John L. "The Education Explosion: Foreign Student Enrollments in the United States," Overseas, II (March, 1963), 2-5.

    The author discusses the growing competition between foreign and American students as both vie for entry to American universities. Statistical information is included.

446. Trent, W. J., Jr. "United Negro College Fund's African Scholarship Program," Journal of Negro Education, XXXI (Spring, 1962), 205-9.

447. United States Medical Training for Foreign Students and Physicians. New York: Committee on Educational Interchange Policy, Institute of International Education, 1957. Pp. 16. (Out of print.)

    The pamphlet is subtitled, "A Discussion of the Problems of the Education and Training of Foreign Medical Personnel in the United States." The statistics are dated, but the discussion of problems involved remains of contemporary interest.

448. University of Hawaii, Department of Sociology. The Evaluations of the Japanese and Thai Grantees of Their Orientation Experiences. Part II. Washington, D.C.: Bureau of Educational and Cultural Affairs, United States Department of State, 1955. Pp. 58.

449. _____. Reactions of Asiatic Grantees to Orientation in Hawaii. Part I. Washington, D.C.: Bureau of Educational and Cultural Affairs, United States Department of State, 1954. Pp. 41.

450. WHO Post-Basic Nursing Education Programmes for Foreign Students. Report of a Conference, Oct. 5-19, 1959. ("World Health Organization Technical Department Series," No. 199.) Geneva, Switzerland: The Organization, 1960. Pp. 47.

451. Walton, Barbara J., and Leavy, Sylvia S. "How Long Do Foreign Students Study in the United States?," *Institute of International Education: News Bulletin*, XXXIII (April, 1958), 21-25.

452. Ward, Douglas S. "In Awarding Scholarships to Latin America--Let's Discriminate!," *Phi Delta Kappan*, XLVII (January, 1966), 269-70.

453. Williams, David B. "Development of Effective Academic Programs for Foreign Students; Curricular, Work Experience, and Social Aspects." ("IAD Mimeograph," No. 5.) Office of International Agricultural Development, New York State College of Agriculture, Ithaca, 1964. Pp. 12.

454. Williams, E. I. F. "Foreign Students in the United States," *Educational Forum*, XXIV (November, 1959), 29-31.

455. Williams, Herbert H. *Foreign Study for Syrians; A Guide to a Long Range Program*. ("Occasional Paper," No. 4.) New York: Institute of International Education, 1953. Pp. 67.

456. _____. *Syrians Studying Abroad: A Comparison of Factors Influencing the Number of Syrians Studying in the United States and Other Countries*. ("Occasional Paper," No. 2.) New York: Institute of International Education, 1952. Pp. 20.

*457. *Women in Educational Exchange with the Developing Countries*. New York: Committee on Educational Interchange Policy, Institute of International Education, 1963.

Women in most countries participate in "academic exchange programs in numbers roughly proportionate to their representation in higher education at home. United States selection processes for women are no different . . . /from/ those for men, but discrimination occurs in their own social and educational systems prior to application." A number of recommendations are made for the future, including the development of programs for women leaders and specialists, and increased attention to women in semiprofessional fields.

458. Woodyatt, Philip C. "We Are So Kind . . . ," *International House Quarterly*, XIX (Winter, 1955), 10-15.

Woodyatt claims that American fretting and trying to reduce "cultural shock" in foreign students may in fact aggravate the problem by unconscious efforts to convert them to the values of our society.

ATTITUDES AND ADJUSTMENT

Several program evaluations found in the section "Foreign Students: Alumni, Returnees, and Program Evaluations," especially those of the Exchange-of-Persons Program, pertain also to this topic. Literature devoted specifically to counseling foreign students will be found in the preceding section, "Foreign Students: Philosophy, Curricula, and Organization."

459. Bardis, P. D. "Social Distance Among Foreign Students," *Sociology and Social Research*, XLI (November, 1956), 112-14.

*460. Beals, Ralph L., and Humphrey, Norman D. *No Frontier to Learning; The Mexican Student in the United States*. Sponsored by the Committee on Cross-Cultural Education of the Social Science Research Council. Minneapolis: University of Minnesota Press, 1957. Pp. 148.

Extensive interviews, questionnaires, and case studies provide the data. An important departure from most studies of foreign students is the authors' attempt to understand the students' reactions to American culture by closely examining their home culture and attitudes.

461. Bennett, John W., and McKnight, Robert K. "Liberation or Alienation: The Japanese Woman Student in America," *Institute of International Education: News Bulletin*, XXXI (April, 1956), 38-47.

462. _____, and _____. "Misunderstandings in Communication Between Japanese Students and Americans," *Social Problems*, III (April, 1956), 243-56.

*463. _____, _____, and Passin, Herbert. *In Search of Identity: The Japanese Overseas Scholar in America and Japan.* Sponsored by the Committee on Cross-Cultural Education of the Social Science Research Council. Minneapolis: University of Minnesota Press, 1958. Pp. 369.

Studying the problem of identity, the authors concentrate on the Japanese student in the new cultural environment of the United States and his relation to cultural and historical changes in Japanese society. The first part of the study takes place at an American university, the second and major part in Japan with people educated in the United States. An extensive methodological appendix is included.

464. _____, _____, and _____. "The Japanese Overseas Student," *Institute of International Education: News Bulletin,* XXXI (January, 1956), 30-34.

465. Coan, Clark. *A Study of International Students Attending the University of Kansas Concerning Some Selected Opinions and Attitudes About the United States, Its Educational System, and Particularly That of the Attended Institution, 1961-62.* ("International Student Studies Series," No. 7.) Lawrence: University of Kansas, 1963. Available from the author, Foreign Student Adviser, University of Kansas.

*466. Coelho, George V. *Changing Images of America: A Study of Indian Students' Perceptions.* Glencoe, Ill.: Free Press, 1958. Pp. 145.

The hypothesis, later substantiated, which guided the research was that "a foreign student's orientation to his reference groups in the host culture would show increasingly differentiated responses with increasing length of sojourn." Attitudes toward the host culture are discussed in terms of four time phases.

*467. _____ (ed.). "Impacts of Studying Abroad," *Journal of Social Issues,* XVIII,1 (1962), entire issue.

Essays on attitude formation in cross-cultural education: "Factors Influencing Attitudes of

Foreign Students Toward the Host Country," Claire Selltiz and Stuart W. Cook; "Informational and Non-Informational Determinants of Nationality Stereotypes," Ake Bjerstedt; "The Effects of a Year's Experience in America on the Self-Image of Scandinavians: A Preliminary Analysis of Reactions to a New Environment," Lotte Bailyn and Herbert C. Kelman; "The Foreign Student, as Stranger, Learning the Norms of the Host Culture," Erling O. Schild; "Personal Growth and Educational Development Through Working and Studying Abroad," George V. Coelho; "Changing Attitudes Through International Activities," Herbert C. Kelman.

468. Cook, David R. "The Indian Student Analyzed," Overseas, III (January, 1964), 9-13.

469. Cook, Stuart W., and Selltiz, Claire. "Some Factors Which Influence the Attitudinal Outcomes of Personal Contact," International Social Science Bulletin, VII,1 (1955), 51-58.

470. Davis, James M., Hanson, Russell G., and Burnor, Duane R. Survey of the African Student: His Achievements and His Problems. New York: Institute of International Education, 1961. Pp. 71.

471. Dean, James W. Adjustment of International Students to the Virginia Polytechnic Institute Campus. Blacksburg: Virginia Polytechnic Institute, 1961. Pp. 37.

472. Diab, Lutfy N. "Authoritarianism and Prejudice in Near-Eastern Students Attending American Universities," Journal of Social Psychology, L (1959), 175-87.

473. DuBois, Cora. Foreign Students and Higher Education in the United States. (See No. 388.)

474. _____. "Motivations of Students Coming to the United States," Institute of International Education: News Bulletin, XXIX (June, 1954), 2-7.

475. _____. "Some Notions on Learning Intercultural Understanding" in Education and Anthropology. Ed. George Dearborn Spindler. Stanford, Calif.: Stanford University, 1955. Pp. 302.

476. Forstat, Reisha. "Adjustment Problems of International Students," *Sociology and Social Research*, XXXVI (September, 1951), 25-30.

477. French, John R. P., Jr., and Zajonc, Robert B. "An Experimental Study of Cross-Cultural Norm Conflict," *Journal of Abnormal and Social Psychology*, LIV (March, 1957), 218-24.

478. Gannon, Martin, and Shively, Stanley E. *Anticipated Changes in Communist Nations*. Washington, D.C.: Air Force Office of Scientific Research, United States Department of Defense, 1962.

   Part of the *Comparative Impact on Attitudes of Actual Versus Anticipated Events*. (See No. 504.)

479. Gezi, Khalil Ismail. *Acculturation of Middle Eastern Arab Students in Selected American Colleges and Universities*. Washington, D.C.: American Friends of the Middle East, 1959. Pp. 102.

480. Green, Walter. "German Exchange Students in the United States--A Case Study," *Human Organization*, XIII (Fall, 1954), 16-22.

481. Haller, A. D., and Bray, Barbara. "Attitudes of American Students Differentially Liked by Latin American Students," *Personnel and Guidance Journal*, XXXVIII (November, 1959), 217-21.

   A bibliography is included.

482. Hauch, Charles C. *Foreign Understanding and Interpretation of United States Education*. Report on a Conference at the United States Office of Education. ("Studies in Comparative Education," OE-14059.) Washington, D.C.: Office of Education, United States Department of Health, Education and Welfare, 1960. Pp. 30.

   Discussion centered on general considerations, expectations of foreign nationals coming to the United States, and recognition of United States educational experience. Of special concern was the lower ranking given to United States degrees compared to similar degrees in other countries.

483. Kelman, Herbert C., and Bailyn, Lotte. "Effects of Cross-Cultural Experience on National Images: A Study of Scandinavian Students in America," *Journal of Conflict Resolution*, VI (December, 1962), 319-34.

484. Kiell, Norman. "Attitudes of Foreign Students," *Journal of Higher Education*, XXII (April, 1951), 188-225. Condensed in *Institute of International Education: News Bulletin*, XXVII (April, 1952), 32-33.

485. Klinger, M. R. B. "Moral Values Across Cultures: A Factorial Study," *Personnel and Guidance Journal*, XLI (October, 1962), 139-43.

486. Krueger, Anna Barbara. "Analysis of Programs, Attitudes, and Reactions to the American Experience of 124 German Youth and Community Leaders." Report, 1951, International Exchange Project. Mimeo., Education-Recreation Division, National Social Welfare Assembly, 1952. Pp. 96.

*487. Lambert, Richard D. (ed.). "America Through Foreign Eyes," *The Annals*, CCXCV (September, 1954), entire issue.

Seven of the fourteen essays are concerned with how foreign students see Americans: "Indian Students and the United States: Cross-Cultural Images," Richard D. Lambert and Marvin Bressler; "Images of the United States and Britain Held by Foreign-Educated Indians," Ruth H. and John Useem; "The American-Educated Japanese, I and II," Herbert Passin and John W. Bennett; "The Mexican Student Views the United States," Ralph L. Beals; "The Mexican Image of Americans," Norman D. Humphrey; "Scandinavian Students' Images of the United States: A Study in Cross-Cultural Education," William H. Sewell, Richard T. Morris, and Oluf M. Davidsen; "The Swedish Students' Image of the United States," Franklin D. Scott.

*488. _____, and Bressler, Marvin. *Indian Students on an American Campus*. Sponsored by the Committee on Cross-Cultural Education of the Social Science Research Council. Minneapolis: University of Minnesota Press, 1956. Pp. 122.

A sample of nineteen South Asian students was interviewed over a period of one year on an American campus. The research hypothesis was that the main determinants of the students' behavior lay in Indian culture and in personal histories. Methodological concentration was on the "role"; three were singled out--student, tourist, and unofficial ambassador. The carefully structured variables yield important information on the students' adjustment to the American experience and their attitudes toward the United States and its people. An effort was made to combine findings with The Western-Educated Man in India by John and Ruth H. Useem. (See No. 647.)

489. _____, and _____. "The Sensitive Area Complex: A Contribution to the Theory of Guided Culture Contact," American Journal of Sociology, LX (May, 1955), 583-92.

490. Lippitt, Ronald, and Watson, Jeanne. "Cross-Culture Learning: A Study Among a Group of German Leaders," Institute of International Education: News Bulletin, XXX (June, 1955), 2-5.

491. _____, and _____. "Some Special Problems of Learning and the Teaching Process in Cross-Cultural Education." (See No. 412.)

492. Long, Lewis M. K. "An Image of America," Journal of Higher Education, XXIX (January, 1958), 31-37.

The author examines the changing attitudes of Brazilian students toward democracy during and following their stays in America. Conclusions reached are: (a) The democratic orientation of the student's personality increases although this may not be detected until his return to Brazil. (b) Democracy and America are seen in a more favorable light. (c) The student usually becomes more critical of his home country. A bibliography is included.

493. Loomis, Charles P., and Schuler, Edgar A. "Acculturation of Foreign Students in the United States," Applied Anthropology, VII (Spring, 1948), 17-34.

Name of publication is now Human Organization.

*494. Lundstedt, Sven (ed.). "Human Factors in Cross-Cultural Adjustment," _Journal of Social Issues_, XIX (July, 1963), entire issue.

Essays on cross-cultural adjustment: "An Introduction to Some Evolving Problems in Cross-Cultural Research," Sven Lundstedt; "A Factorial Study of Morale Among Peace Corps Teachers in Ghana," M. Brewster Smith, et al.; "An Extension of the U-Curve Hypothesis," John T. and Jeanne E. Gullahorn; "African Students in the United States," Joseph Veroff; "The Reactions of Participants in a Foreign Specialists Seminar to Their American Experience," Herbert C. Kelman; "Some Factors in the Adjustment of Foreign Nationals in the United States," Steven E. Deutsch and George Y. M. Won; "Sojourn Research: A Definition of the Field," Eugene H. Jacobson.

495. Lysgaard, Sverre. "Adjustment in a Foreign Society: Norwegian Fulbright Grantees Visiting the United States," _International Social Science Bulletin_, VII,1 (1955), 45-51.

496. McClintock, Charles G., and Davis, James M. "Changes in the Attributes of 'Nationality' in the Self-Percept of the 'Stranger'," _Journal of Social Psychology_, XLVIII (November, 1958), 183-93.

497. Marquardt, William F. (ed.). _The Foreign Student Speaks_. Seattle: University of Washington, 1958. Pp. 129.

A collection of essays.

498. Marsh, Gayle G., and Halberstam, Jacob L. "Personality Stereotypes of United States and Foreign Medical Residents," _Journal of Social Psychology_, LXVIII (April, 1966), 187-96.

499. Melby, John F., and Wolf, Elinor K. _Looking Glass for Americans: A Study of the Foreign Students at the University of Pennsylvania_. Philadelphia: National Council on Asian Affairs, 1961. Pp. 51.

500. Mills, Richard C. _Narrow Is the Road: Cultural Forces Affecting the Emotional Adjustment of Students from Southeast Asia to the_

American Campus Community. Los Angeles: Custom Publishers, 1963. Available from the Clairmore Fund.

501. Milstein, Elliott, Chunn, Anthony F., and Dole, Arthur A. "Why They Came to Graduate School: A Comparison of Foreign and American Students," Social Process, XXVI (1963), 27-41.

502. Mischel, Walter. "German Exchange Students at Ohio State University: An Analysis of Responses to an Incomplete Sentence Test." ("Studies in German-American Post War Problems," No. 4.) Columbus: Ohio State University, 1957.

*503. Morris, Richard T., and Davidsen, Oluf M. The Two-Way Mirror; National Status in Foreign Students' Adjustment. Minneapolis: University of Minnesota Press, 1960. Pp. 215.

Believing that the international status of the foreign student's country becomes an important new personality variable when he enters the United States, the authors examine its relation to the student's attitudes toward the United States. The problem of personal adjustment to the new environment is also thoroughly discussed. A bibliography is included.

504. Nehnevjsa, J. Comparative Impact of Attitudes of Actual Versus Anticipated Events. Washington, D.C.: Air Force Office of Scientific Research, United States Department of Defense, 1965.

Foreign graduate student reactions to East-West bloc differences are studied to generate a theory of foreign-elite reaction.

505. Nielsen, Waldemar A., Bryant, William Cullen, II, and Wyatt, Donald W. "Our African Students," Overseas, I (February, 1962), 14-18.

This article is a critique of the methodology involved in the Survey of the African Student: His Achievements and His Problems. (See No. 470.) The author particularly attacks the reliability of evidence demonstrating African-American Negro friction.

506. 1960 Survey of International Students at the University of Michigan. (Project 1160). Ann Arbor: Survey Research Center, University of Michigan, 1961. Pp. 11.

    A bibliography is included.

507. Olsen, Lionel R., and Kunhart, William E. "Foreign Student Reactions to American College Life," Journal of Educational Sociology, XXXI (March, 1958), 277-80.

508. Pedram, Manouchehr. An Analysis of the Reactions of Foreign Students Attending the University of Kansas Concerning the American Educational Process and Procedure. ("International Student Studies Series," No. 2.) Lawrence: University of Kansas, 1960.

509. Rathore, Naeem G. The Pakistan Student. New York: American Friends of the Middle East, Inc., 1958. Pp. 69.

    The author examines the Pakistani student's desire to study in the United States, his preconceptions of it, his problems, and his evaluation of the experience. A bibliography is included.

510. Rettig, Salomon, and Pasamanick, Benjamin. "Moral Codes of American and Foreign Academic Intellectuals in an American University," Journal of Social Psychology, LI (May, 1960), 229-44.

511. _____, and _____. "Moral Codes of American and Korean College Students," Journal of Social Psychology, L (August, 1959), 65-73.

512. _____, and Rawson, Harve E. "The Risk Hypothesis in Predictive Judgments of Unethical Behavior," Journal of Abnormal and Social Psychology, LXVI (1963), 243-48. Also a paper presented at the 57th Annual Meeting of the American Sociological Association, Washington, D.C., August, 1962.

513. _____, and Singh, Paras N. "Cross-Cultural Differences in Habitual Response Preferences as an Index of Anxiety," Journal of Social Psychology, LVIII (October, 1962), 9-15.

514. Riegel, Oscar W. "Residual Effects of Exchange of Persons," <u>Public Opinion Quarterly</u>, XVII (Fall, 1953), 319-27.

    Data are collected from an investigation of former Belgian student exchangees. Summarizing, the author finds the immediate reaction to the experience was enthusiastic, with correspondingly favorable attitudes towards the United States. As time passes, the residual effect is one of warm friendliness toward particular Americans, but the exchangees do not retain social and political attitudes more favorable to the United States than non-exchangees.

515. Rose, Arnold M. "Some Consequences of Brief Cultural Contact," <u>Phylon</u>, XIV (June, 1953), 125-33.

516. Sasnett, Martena T. (ed.). <u>Foreign Students Look at the U.S.</u> With the cooperation of the National Association of Foreign Student Advisers. Los Angeles: Cole-Holmquist Press, 1960.

517. Scott, Franklin D. "Academic Vikings," <u>American Scandinavian Review</u>, XLVII (March, 1959), 54-60.

518. Selby, Henry A., and Woods, Clyde M. "Foreign Students at a High-Pressure University," <u>Sociology of Education</u>, XXXIX (Spring, 1966), 138-54.

519. Selltiz, Claire. <u>Comparison of Findings of Studies of Foreign Students in France and the U.S.</u> New York: Research Center for Human Relations, New York University, 1962.

520. _____. "Social Contacts of Foreign Students with Americans," excerpts from "Attitudes and Social Relations of Foreign Students in the United States" in <u>School and Society</u>, XC (Summer, 1963), 261-66.

    A bibliography is included.

*521. _____, Cook, Stuart W., and Christ, June R. <u>Attitudes and Social Relations of Foreign Students in the United States</u>. Minneapolis: University of Minnesota Press, 1963. Pp. 434.

The question of attitude change of national groups as a result of intergroup contact provides the study's focus. The authors investigated (a) environmental factors influencing social relations of foreign students and their hosts, (b) the effect of these relations on the foreign student's attitudes toward the host country and its people, and (c) the effects of a preliminary orientation program on alleviating problems of transition. The sample includes 375 students and numerous American institutions where they studied. Several interesting comparisons with findings of other Social Science Research Council studies are made. A methodological appendix and bibliography are included.

*522. Sewell, William H., and Davidsen, Oluf M. Scandinavian Students on an American Campus. Sponsored by the Committee on Cross-Cultural Education of the Social Science Research Council. Minneapolis: University of Minnesota Press, 1961. Pp. 134.

The study invites a comparison with studies of students from cultures which differ more than does the Scandinavian from the culture of the United States. The purposes of the study are (a) to gather information on social and academic adjustment; (b) to discover attitudes toward the United States and their change over time; (c) to examine the relation of background, intellectual attainment, and socio-political orientation to impressions of America and personal adjustment (which perhaps yielded the most significant results in the study); and (d) to provide suggestions for the conduct of future student-exchange programs. Explanations of data and methodology are included.

523. Shaffer, Robert H., and Dowling, Leo R. "Foreign Students and Their American Student Friends." ("Cooperative Research Project," No. 5-0806.) Mimeo., Indiana University, 1966. Pp. 367. A summary form of the study is also available.

A detailed report on the nature of foreign-American student interaction at Indiana University, this study concentrates on the presentation of the characteristics of American students named as friends by foreign students. A review of relevant literature, a description of the methodology, numerous conclusions, several recommendations for school policy, and an extensive bibliography are included.

524. Shively, Stanley E. Perceived Economic and Military Strength of Nations. Washington, D.C.: Air Force Office of Scientific Research, United States Department of Defense, 1962.

    Part of the Comparative Impact on Attitudes of Actual Versus Anticipated Events. (See No. 504.)

*525. Smith, M. Brewster (ed.). "Attitudes and Adjustment in Cross-Cultural Contact: Recent Studies of Foreign Students," Journal of Social Issues, XII,1 (1956), entire issue.

    Several of these essays are derived from research sponsored by the Committee on Cross-Cultural Education of the Social Science Research Council. Contributions include "The Adjustment of Scandinavian Students," William H. Sewell and Oluf M. Davidsen; "National Status and Attitudes of Foreign Students," Richard T. Morris; "Factors Associated with the Development of Cross-Cultural Social Interaction," Rose K. Goldsen, Edward A. Suchman, and Robin M. Williams, Jr.; "The Effects of Situation Factors on Personal Interaction Between Foreign Students and Americans," Claire Selltiz, Anna Lee Hopson, and Stuart W. Cook; "Perspective for Further Research on Cross-Cultural Education," M. Brewster Smith.

526. _____. "Some Features of Foreign Student Adjustment," Journal of Higher Education, XXVI (May, 1955), 231-41.

    A bibliography is included.

527. Spencer, Richard E. The Christian and Non-Christian Symbolic Orientation of American and Foreign Students. 1963. Available from the Division of Instructional Services, The Pennsylvania State University, University Park, Pennsylvania.

528. Tanenhaus, Joseph, and Roth, Sidney G. "Non-Immigrant Foreign Students: A Survey of Their Needs and Interests." (See No. 444.)

529. United States Department of State. <u>Preconceptions of Foreign Leaders Visiting the United States for the First Time</u>. New York: Institute of World Affairs, New School for Social Research, 1953. Pp. 166.

530. <u>Views of African Students on Strengthening African-American Relations</u>. Washington, D.C.: Institute of African-American Relations, 1956. Pp. 39.

531. Walton, D. Michael. <u>Anticipated Change of Non-Communist Nations Toward Communism</u>. Washington, D.C.: Air Force Office of Scientific Research, United States Department of Defense, 1962.

Part of the <u>Comparative Impact on Attitudes of Actual Versus Anticipated Events</u>. (See No. 504.)

532. _____. <u>Explorations in Personal and National Efficacy</u>. Washington, D.C.: Air Force Office of Scientific Research, United States Department of Defense, January, 1962.

Part of the <u>Comparative Impact on Attitudes of Actual Versus Anticipated Events</u>. (See No. 504.)

533. Watson, Jeanne, and Lippitt, Ronald. <u>Learning Across Cultures: A Study of Germans Visiting America</u>. (Pub. No. 4.) Ann Arbor: Research Center for Group Dynamics, Institute for Social Research, University of Michigan, 1955. Pp. 205.

The authors discuss the attitudes of Germans during and after their stays in America. A group of Americans were given the identical tests administered to the Germans in order to note initial attitude discrepancies between visitor and host that would be a stimulus to cross-cultural learning. Areas of inquiry included ideas about Germany and America, democracy, social change, and family relationships.

534. Wheatley, Charles W. <u>Comparative Study of Personal and Perceived National Ideologies</u>. Washington, D.C.: Air Force Office of Scientific Research, United States Department of Defense, 1961.

Part of the <u>Comparative Impact on Attitudes of Actual Versus Anticipated Events</u>. (See No. 504.)

535. Wilder, Emilia. "America as Seen by Polish Exchange Scholars," <u>Public Opinion Quarterly</u>, XXVIII (Summer, 1964), 243-56.

536. Zajonc, Robert B. "Aggressive Attitudes of the 'Stranger' as a Function of Conformity Pressures," <u>Human Relations</u>, V (1952), 205-16.

ADMISSION AND CREDENTIAL EVALUATION

537. "Admission and Placement of Foreign Undergraduate Students; Panel Discussion," <u>College and University</u>, XL (Summer, 1965), 429-32.

538. Angell, Melvin. "A Descriptive Analysis of the Academic Achievement of Selected Samples of Foreign Students from Non-English Speaking Countries at Fresno State College," Ditto, Student Personnel Services Test Office, Fresno State College, 1960. Pp. 13.

539. Bowles, Frank H. <u>Access to Higher Education: The International Study of University Admissions</u>. New York: International Documents Service, Columbia University Press, 1963.

540. Catlin, Louella C. "Comparison of the Achievement of Foreign and Non-Foreign College Students," <u>Journal of College Student Personnel</u>, IV (October, 1962), 28-31.

541. Cooper, Robert L., and Stieglitz, Francine B. "The English Proficiency of Foreign Students at Columbia University," <u>Journal of Higher Education</u>, XXXVI (March, 1965), 131-36.

542. Dembo, Miriam. "Pre-Screening of Foreign

Students to Reduce Dropouts," College and University, XL (Winter, 1965), 140-44.

543. Diamond, Lorraine K., and Lorge, Irving. "The English Proficiency of Foreign Students," Journal of Higher Education, XXV (January, 1954), 19-26.

544. Dizney, Henry F., and Roskens, Ronald W. "Comparative Aptitude and Achievement of American and Foreign Students in an American University," Journal of College Student Personnel, V (March, 1964), 146-51.

*545. The Foreign Student: Whom Shall We Welcome? Report of the Study Committee on Foreign Student Affairs. New York: Education and World Affairs, 1964. Pp. 35.

Addressed to all universities and agencies involved in international student exchanges, the study is specifically concerned with the guiding, screening, and selecting of foreign students. The following topics are examined: overseas centers to improve the selection process, the role of foreign students in American colleges and universities, the responsibilities of government and private agencies, and the general problems of undergraduate and graduate admission. Ralph W. Tyler was chairman of the committee.

546. Gouverneur, Isabel M. A Guide to the Evaluation of Venezuelan Academic Credentials. Caracas: Education Committee of the North American Association of Venezuela, March, 1955.

547. Hountras, Peter Timothy. "Academic Probation Among Foreign Graduate Students," School and Society, LXXXIV (September 1, 1956), 75-77.

548. _____. "Factors Related to Academic Probation Among Foreign Graduate Students," School and Society, LXXXV (October 26, 1957), 311-12.

549. _____. "The Relationship Between the Pre-Admission Data and Achievement of Foreign Graduate Students," Journal of Educational Psychology, XLVIII (March, 1957), 157-63.

550. Kaulfers, Walter V. "Pitfalls in Comparing Foreign Schools with Ours," Educational Record, XLIV (July, 1963), 275-87.

This article urges that more accurate school comparisons be made. Seven central questions are postulated: (a) Are differences in terminology considered? (b) What age groups are being compared? (c) Have the many distinct types of schools for teen-agers abroad been taken into account? (d) At what price in failure of students are the presumably superior standards of education abroad maintained? (e) How easy is the native language to learn to read, write, and spell? (f) How long is the school week and year? (g) How satisfied are foreign countries with their schools?

551. Koenig, Clara H. "The Evaluation of Credentials from Foreign Countries," College and University, XXVII (October, 1951), 14-28.

552. _____. "The Scholastic Performance of Foreign Students in the United States," College and University, XXVIII (January, 1953), 189-96.

553. Mulligan, Agnes C. "Evaluating Foreign Credentials," College and University, XLI (Spring, 1966), 307-13.

*554. The Overseas Selection of Foreign Students. New York: Education and World Affairs, 1966. Pp. 34.

"The report's principal objective is to consider how the crucial and essential first steps--counseling, evaluating, and testing--can be carried out in a manner helpful both to the student and to his teachers and hosts in this country." Inquiries of officials were made both in this country and overseas. Numerous explicit recommendations are suggested.

555. "Research on Foreign Student Admissions--Japan; Panel Discussion," College and University, XL (Summer, 1965), 433-34.

556. "Research Papers from the 1964 Seminar on Asian Cultures." Mimeo., National Association for Foreign Student Affairs, 1964.

Papers included are: "The English Proficiency of Foreign Students at Columbia University," Robert L. Cooper and Francine B. Stieglitz; "The Academic Success of New Chinese Graduate Students," Denise Hawkins; "Predicting Scholastic Performance of Hong Kong Students Applying for Admission to Undergraduate Colleges and Universities of the United States," Clifford Sjogren; "The Comparative Attitude Towards Americans Abroad by Foreign Students and Americans," Richard Spencer.

*557. Sasnett, Martena T. (ed.). A Guide to the Admission and Placement of Foreign Students. 2nd ed. ("World Education Series.") With the cooperation of the American Association of Collegiate Registrars and Admissions Officers. New York: Institute of International Education, 1962.

558. _____. "Updating Foreign Student Admissions," College and University, XXXIX (Fall, 1963), 13-24.

*559. Strain, William H. (ed.). Guides to the Academic Placement of Students from Foreign Countries in Educational Institutions in the U.S. Washington, D.C.: American Association of Collegiate Registrars and Admissions Officers.

The pamphlet series includes Canada, 1957; Germany, 1957; Korea, 1958; Thailand, 1959; Scandinavian Study Tour, 1959; Netherlands, 1961; Mexico, 1961; Venezuela, 1961; Austria, 1961; Caribbean, 1961; Afghanistan, 1961; Rumania, 1961; Hong Kong, 1961; Tanganyika, 1961; Philippines, 1962; Argentina, 1962; Italy, 1962; United Kingdom, 1963; France, 1964; India, 1964; Czechoslovakia, 1964; Iran, 1964; Poland, 1964; Lebanon, 1964; Switzerland, 1965; Chile, 1965; New Zealand, 1965; Peru, 1965. The following are in press: USSR, Germany, Soviet Zone of Germany, Japan, and Iraq.

560. _____. "Selection and Admission of Foreign Students," Liberal Education, XLVIII (March, 1962), 77-83.

561. _____. "Which Foreign Students Should U.S.

Institutions Admit?," *Phi Delta Kappan*, XLVI (March, 1965), 332-35.

The author briefly discusses problems involving sponsoring groups and credential evaluation and concludes with a comment on the Education and World Affairs Report, *The Foreign Student: Whom Shall We Welcome?* (see No. 545), suggesting that the report failed to recognize the commendable admission practices now in operation.

*562. _____, and Arnold, Ruth. *Do-It-Yourself Evaluation of Foreign Student Credentials*. Rev. ed. Washington, D.C.: American Association of Collegiate Registrars and Admissions Officers, in press.

563. *Student Records from Vietnam: Their Evaluation for Placement of Students in American Educational Institutions*. Washington, D.C.: United States Operations Mission to Vietnam, 1962.

564. Thompson, Ronald Burdick. "Academic Records of Foreign Students," *College and University*, XXVII (October, 1951), 29-33.

*565. *U.S. College and University Policies, Practices, and Problems in Admitting Foreign Students*. New York: Institute of International Education, 1965.

CHAPTER 12   TRAINING FOREIGN SPECIALISTS IN THE UNITED STATES

This chapter notes items pertaining to the United States education of foreign specialists--usually those involved in development activity. Also relevant to this topic are several evaluations of government "participant" programs cited in the following chapter.

566. Israel, Thomas S. "Administrative Training of Foreign Officials in the United States," International Review of Administrative Sciences, XXIII (1957), 26-30.

*567. Lesser, Simon O., and Peter, Hollis W. "Training Foreign Nationals in the United States" in Some Applications of Behavioural Research. Ed. Rensis Likert and Samuel P. Hayes, Jr. ("Science and Society," No. 2; UNESCO SS.56.X.2A.) Paris: United Nations Educational, Scientific, and Cultural Organization, 1957, pp. 160-206.

   An evaluation and summary of research which concentrates on academic environment rather than on industrial and business situations. The objectives and importance of training programs are critically discussed. A lengthy examination of the factors affecting the success of training programs is included.

568. Maddox, James G., and Tolley, Howard R. Case Studies of Training Through Technical Cooperation. Washington, D.C.: National Planning Association, 1957. Pp. 81.

   The bilateral technical-cooperation training programs between the United States and Latin America are the subjects of this thorough study. The history of the programs, case studies, an evaluation, and several recommendations are included--all of which are pertinent to continuing discussions of training programs.

569. Schlesinger, Ben. "American Training for Indian Social Worker: Cure or Curse?," Indian Journal of Social Work, XXI (December, 1960), 261-65.

570. Thurber, Clarence E. "Training Administrators for Developing Countries; A Survey and Suggestions," International Development Review, III (June, 1961), 34-38.

*571. _____, and Weidner, Edward W. Technical Assistance in Training Administrators: Lessons from the American Experience. ("Selected Papers on Public Administration," No. 2.) Bloomington: Institute of Training for Public Service, Department of Government, Indiana University, 1962.

Each of the authors contributes a paper: Thurber, "Lessons from Efforts to Train Foreign Administrators in the United States," and Weidner, "The American Education of Foreign Administrators: Lessons from American Training Programs in Foreign Countries."

572. Training for Leadership and Service: Proceedings of the National Conference on the International Training Programs of AID, June 25-26, 1962. Washington, D.C.: International Training Division, Agency for International Development, United States Department of State, 1962. Pp. 88. (Out of print.)

573. Training Foreign Nationals in the United States. Ann Arbor, Mich.: Foundation for Research on Human Behavior, 1956. Pp. 36.

This report on a 1954 seminar reflects the practical concerns of the seminar participants from business, government, education, foundations, and research agencies. Topics systematically discussed are: pre-arrival factors (problems of selection, categories of trainees, language facility, at-home orientation programs), sojourn factors (spectator phase, involvement phase, coming-to-terms phase, pre-departure phase, U-shaped curve of adjustment to host country, training trainers, conflict of loyalties to home and to host), and factors upon returning home. Discussion is in terms of program goals that may involve academic or technical training. A bibliography is included.

574. Van Mook, H. J. "Note on Training Abroad in Public Administration for Students from Underdeveloped Countries," International Review of Administrative Sciences, XXVI,1 (1960), 67-69.

575. Waltman, Howard L. "Cross-Cultural Training in Public Administration," Public Administration Review, XXI (Summer, 1961), 141-47.

576. Wharton, Clifton R., Jr. The U.S. Graduate Training of Asian Agricultural Economists. New York: Council on Economic and Cultural Affairs, Inc., 1959. Pp. 57.

CHAPTER **13** ALUMNI, RETURNEES, AND PROGRAM EVALUATIONS

577. American Embassy, Bonn, Germany. <u>Study of Impressions and Disseminations by Information Specialists and Students from the Exchange of Persons Program</u>. Bad Godesberg, Germany: Institut für Sozial- und Wirtschaftsforschung, 1955. Pp. 48.

578. American Embassy, New Delhi, India. <u>The Exchange of Persons: An Evaluation of the Experience and Training of Indian Grantees under Fulbright and Technical Cooperation Programs</u>. Washington, D.C.: Bureau of Educational and Cultural Affairs, United States Department of State, 1953. Pp. 93.

579. American Embassy, Vienna, Austria. <u>Report on a Survey of the Department of State Exchange of Persons Program in Austria</u>. Washington, D.C.: Bureau of Educational and Cultural Exchange, United States Department of State, 1955. Pp. 190.

580. American Institute for Research, Inc. <u>A Pilot Study of Participant Training in the United States</u>. 2 vols. Washington, D.C.: Agency for International Development, United States Department of State, June, 1963. Vol. I, <u>Executive Report</u>. Pp. 28. Vol. II, <u>Technical Report</u>. Pp. 56.

581. Andrews, Wade H., and Miller, Walter W. "A Survey of the Impact of the International Farm Youth Exchange Program at the Ohio State University." ("Dept. Mimeograph Bulletin in Rural Sociology.") Mimeo., Department of Agricultural

Economics and Rural Sociology, Ohio State University, 1956. Pp. 28.

582. Asthana, Hari S., et al. Indo-American Participant Training Program--An Evaluation Study. New Delhi, India: Training Section, United States Technical Cooperation Mission to India, International Cooperation Administration, United States Department of State, 1959. Pp. 56.

583. Barakat, Mohamed Khalifa, et al. Studies on the Role as Culture Carriers of Eastern Students Who Received Their University Education in Western Countries: Report on the United Arab Republic's Study. (UNESCO SS/COM/6.) Paris: United Nations Educational, Scientific, and Cultural Organization, 1964.

Unanalyzed data gathered from a sample of 187 United Arab Republic students who received training abroad in the United States, United Kingdom, and West Germany. Information is classified according to the following: (a) specific difficulties of the student's adjustment during his sojourn abroad and after his return home, (b) the transmission of information to the host country and home country, (c) impact of the sojourn on the student's personality, and (d) personal background of the student.

584. Bennett, John W. "Innovative Potential of American-Educated Japanese," Human Organization, XXI (Winter, 1962-63), 246-51.

585. Bennington College, Bennington, Vermont. An Inquiry into the Effects of European Student Exchange. Washington, D.C.: Bureau of Educational and Cultural Affairs, United States Department of State, 1958. Pp. 177.

586. Bharagava, K. P. Return Grantee Survey /India/. (IRS. IND. 127.) Washington, D.C.: United States Information Agency, 1961.

587. Bigman, Stanley K. Foreign Journalists See the United States: An Analysis of Articles Published as the Result of a Tour Arranged in

Conjunction with TWA. Study sponsored by the United States Department of State. Washington, D.C.: Bureau of Social Science Research, Inc., 1953.

588. Bolivian Institute of Public Opinion Research, La Paz, Bolivia. *A Study of Former Bolivian Grantees in the United States*. Washington, D.C.: Bureau of Educational and Cultural Affairs, United States Department of State, 1959. Pp. 94.

589. Bonilla, Frank, and Wilson, Elmo C. "Evaluating Exchange of Persons Programs," *Public Opinion Quarterly*, XIX (Spring, 1955), 20-30.

590. Bremseth, Cameron F. *An Evaluation of the Participant Program in Taiwan*. Taipeh, Taiwan: Mutual Security Mission to China, International Cooperation Administration, United States Department of State, 1959. Pp. 81.

591. _____. *Follow-Up Evaluation Study of Iranian Participants Who Received Training in the United States Under ICA Sponsorship*. Washington, D.C.: Operations Mission to Iran, International Cooperation Administration, United States Department of State, 1956. Pp. 43.

592. Bureau of Social Science Research, Inc. *The AID Participant Training Program in Sudan: An Evaluation Study*. Washington, D.C.: Agency for International Development, United States Department of State, 1963. Pp. 121.

593. _____. *An Analysis of Attitude Change Among German Exchangees*. Washington, D.C.: Bureau of Educational and Cultural Affairs, United States Department of State, 1951. Pp. 126.

594. _____. *Cross-Cultural Education and Its Impact*. (See No. 354.)

595. _____. *Foreign Exchange Students Review Their Stay in the United States*. 2 vols. Washington, D.C.: Bureau of Educational and Cultural Affairs, United States Department of State, 1953.

Part I. An Analysis of First Semester Reports, Academic Year 1951-52. Pp. 75.

Part II. An Analysis of Second Semester Reports, Academic Year 1951-52. Pp. 90.

596. _____. The Participant Training Program in Costa Rica. San Jose, Costa Rica: United States AID Mission to Costa Rica, Agency for International Development, United States Department of State, 1963. Pp. 116.

597. _____. Report on Evaluation Survey of Participant Training /Brazil/. Washington, D.C.: Agency for International Development, United States Department of State, 1963. Pp. 239.

598. Career Patterns of Foreign Students Who Received the Ph.D. from the University of Michigan, 1941-1961. ("Graduate Study," No. 5.) Ann Arbor: Horace H. Rackham School of Graduate Studies, University of Michigan, 1962. Pp. 128.

599. Central Research Services, Inc. Evaluation Study of Japanese Returned Fulbright Grantees. Tokyo: International Educational Exchange Service, United States Department of State, 1958. Pp. 194.

600. Clements, Forrest E. "Evaluation Survey of the Participant Training Program of the Agency for International Development." Paper presented for the annual meeting of the American Orthopsychiatric Association. Mimeo., Agency for International Development, United States Department of State, 1963.

601. _____, and Gollin, Albert E. Evaluation of the Technical Training Program in United States Foreign Aid. Washington, D.C.: Agency for International Development, United States Department of State, 1964. Pp. 125. (Out of print.)

602. Coan, Clark. A Study of European Alumni of the University of Kansas (1953-54--1960-61)

Concerning Some Selected Opinions, Information, and Attitudes About the United States, Its Educational System and Particularly That of the Attended Institution. ("International Student Studies Series," No. 8.) Lawrence: University of Kansas, 1964.

603. Cullers, Robert M. "The Japanese Fulbright Returnee . . . What Happens to Him After His Return to Japan?" Mimeo., Exchange of Persons Branch, American Embassy, Tokyo, 1961.

604. _____. "Return to Japan," Overseas, II (November, 1962), 20-24.

605. Donahue, Francis M. Greek Fulbright Research Project: A Study in Cross-Cultural Education; Summary Report. Submitted to the Board of International Education, United States Department of State. East Lansing: Michigan State University, 1956. Pp. 143.

606. Duge, Edna. "International Alumni Groups," Overseas, III (December, 1963), 9-11.

607. Educational Services and Research Center, National Institute of Psychology, Tehran, Iran. An Evaluation of USIS Sponsored Programmes in the United States of America for Iranian Participants. (IRS. IRN. 30.) Washington, D.C.: United States Information Agency, 1963. Pp. 96.

608. Evaluation of the Point IV Training Program in Brazil for USOM to Brazil. Rio de Janeiro: Instituto do Pesquisas do Opiniao e Mercado, United States Department of State, 1959. Pp. 95.

609. An Evaluation Study of the Agency for International Development Participant Training Program in Jamaica. Kingston, Jamaica: Agency for International Development, United States Department of State, 1962. Pp. 95 (plus tables).

610. Evaluation Survey of the Korea/U.S. Participant Training Program 1955-60; Final Report. Washington, D.C.: Agency for International

Development, United States Department of State, 1963. Pp. 224.

611. A German Appraisal of the Fulbright Program: A Study Among the German Participants of the Cultural Exchange Between the Federal Republic and U.S.A. Sponsored by the Bureau of Educational and Cultural Affairs, United States Department of State. Frankfurt am Main, Germany: DIVO, 1961. Pp. 202.

612. German Institute for Public Opinion Research. Evaluation of the Exchange Program in West Germany. (HICOG. GYW. E. 200.) Sponsored by the United States Information Agency. Frankfurt am Main, Germany: DIVO, 1954. Pp. 128.

613. Institute for Social Research, Oslo, Norway. A Study of Intercultural Contact: Norwegian Fulbright Grantees Visiting the United States. 2 vols. Washington, D.C.: Bureau of Educational and Cultural Affairs, United States Department of State, 1954. Pp. 344.

614. Institute for Social Studies, University of Helsinki, Finland. Finnish Fellowship Students in the United States. Washington, D.C.: Bureau of Educational and Cultural Affairs, United States Department of State, 1964. Pp. 138.

615. International Institute for Public Opinion and Market Research (EMNID), Bielefeld, Germany. Impressions of State Department Grantees from Burma. Washington, D.C.: Bureau of Educational and Cultural Affairs, United States Department of State, 1961. Pp. 122.

616. International Public Opinion Research, Inc., New York. Evaluation of International Exchange Experiences of Brazilian Grantees. (IEV. BR. 22.) Washington, D.C.: Bureau of Educational and Cultural Affairs, United States Department of State, 1953. Pp. 128.

617. _____. German Exchangees: A Study in Attitude Change. Washington, D.C.: Bureau of Educational and Cultural Exchange, United States Department of State, 1953. Pp. 58.

ALUMNI, RETURNEES, AND PROGRAM EVALUATIONS

618. _____. *Interviews with Twenty Mexican Teachers to Help Evaluate the Teacher Exchange Program.* Washington, D.C.: Bureau of Educational and Cultural Affairs, United States Department of State, 1953. Pp. 95.

619. International Research Associates, Inc. *Italian Exchangees: A Study in Attitude Change and Diffusion.* Washington, D.C.: International Educational Exchange Service, Bureau of Educational and Cultural Affairs, United States Department of State, 1955. Pp. 39.

620. _____. *The Thai Student Exchangee: A Research Report.* Prepared for the International Educational Exchange Service, United States Department of State. Washington, D.C.: Bureau of Educational and Cultural Affairs, The Department, 1955.

621. International Research Associates, Mexico. *Opinions and Attitudes of Mexicans Who Have Participated in the Educational Exchange Program (IES) Since 1952.* Washington, D.C.: Advisory Commission on International Educational and Cultural Affairs, United States Department of State, 1959.

622. _____. *A Study of Reactions to the ICA Exchange Program Among Returned Mexican Grantees.* Service contract with the International Cooperation Administration conducted in Mexico. Washington, D.C.: Bureau of Educational and Cultural Affairs, United States Department of State, 1959. Pp. 128.

623. Keeffe, Emily C., and Converse, Elizabeth. *The Japanese Leaders Program of the Department of the Army: An Evaluative Report on the Program and Its Conduct by the Institute of International Education, 1950-51.* ("Occasional Paper," No. 1.) New York: Research Program, Institute of International Education, 1952. Pp. 109.

*624. Kuppuswamy, B. *Studies on the Role as Culture Carriers of Eastern Students Who Received Their University Education in Western Countries: Report on the Indian Study.* (UNESCO SS/COM/7.)

Paris: United Nations Educational, Scientific, and Cultural Organization, 1964.

Data gathered from a sample of 177 Indian students to

> study the factors involved in the academic and social adjustment of students who go to the three Western countries, the U.S., the U.K. and West Germany, for higher studies and to isolate the main factors involved in their readjustment in the home country on return. It also aims to study the extent to which these students communicate Indian culture to the Western countries and the Western culture to India on return, and the means of communication they used.

The study also affords a comparative glance at successes and failures of government and university policies in three countries.

625. MacCormac, Kenneth. "Keeping in Touch with Returned Grantees," <u>Institute of International Education: News Bulletin</u>, XXXIV (April, 1959), 30-34.

626. Malik, Charles H. "The Foreign Alumnus," <u>Association of American Colleges Bulletin</u>, XXXIX (December, 1953), 611-17.

627. Moore, Forrest G., and Forman, Robert E. <u>The University and Its Foreign Alumni: Maintaining Overseas Contacts</u>. ("Minnesota Studies in Student Personnel Work," No. 13.) Minneapolis: University of Minnesota Press, 1964. Pp. 78.

A bibliography is included.

628. National Council of Applied Economic Research, New Delhi, India. <u>An Appraisal of the Training Program of the United States Agency for International Development in India</u>. Washington, D.C.: Agency for International Development, United States Department of State, 1963. Pp. 230.

629. Niyekawa, Agnes M. "A Follow-Up Study of

Japan Society Fellowship Grantees." Mimeo., Japan Society, Inc., 1961. Pp. 27.

630. Office of Research and Evaluation, U.S. Information Service, Taiwan. "Reactions of Returned Chinese Grantees to the Educational Exchange Program." Mimeo., United States Information Agency, 1961. Pp. 41.

631. Participant Training Program in Bolivia; Final Report of a Training Evaluation Study. Washington, D.C.: Agency for International Development, United States Department of State, 1964. Pp. 180.

632. Peter, Hollis W., and Schlesinger, Lawrence E. Using United States Training in the Philippines--A Follow-Up Survey of Participants. 2 vols. Prepared for the International Cooperation Administration. Ann Arbor: Institute for Social Research, University of Michigan, 1959.

633. Sabrosky, Laurel K. An Analysis of an Evaluation of the International Farm Youth Exchange Project, 1952. ("IFYE Evaluation Report," No. 2.) Washington, D.C.: Federal Extension Service, United States Department of Agriculture, 1954. Pp. 35. (Out of print.)

634. _____. An Evaluation of the Special Indian Section of the International Farm Youth Exchange Project in Pickaway County, Ohio, in 1953. ("IFYE Evaluation Report," No. 3.) Washington, D.C.: Federal Extension Service, United States Department of Agriculture, 1954. Pp. 18.

635. Scott, Franklin D. The American Experience of Swedish Students: Retrospect and Aftermath. Minneapolis: University of Minnesota Press, 1956. Pp. 129.

From open-ended interviews with and questionnaires from a sample of fifty ex-students, the author assesses the lasting value of study abroad. The book is short, lucidly written, and provides a number of explicit conclusions. It is an offering of the Committee on Cross-

Cultural Education of the Social Science Research Council.

636. Smith, Bradford. "European Fulbrighters Back Home," *Institute of International Education: News Bulletin*, XXXIV (April, 1959), 4-12.

637. Smith, Howard P. "Do Intercultural Experiences Affect Attitudes?," *Journal of Abnormal and Social Psychology*, LI (November, 1955), 469-77.

638. _____. "The Effects of Intercultural Experience--A Follow-Up Investigation," *ibid.*, LIV (March, 1957), 266-69.

639. Smith, M. Brewster. "Evaluation of Exchange of Persons," *International Social Science Bulletin*, VI,3 (1955), 387-97.

640. Spence, Ralph B. *Technical Training of Pakistanis in the United States--An Evaluation of the ICA Program 1951-55*. Karachi: Ferozsons, 1957. Pp. 78.

641. Stabler, John B., and Mogannam, E. Theodore. *Follow-Up and Evaluation Study of Returned International Cooperation Administration Participants in Egypt Who Have Received Training in the United States*. Conducted by the United States Operations Mission to Egypt, Training Staff and Cooperating USOM/Egypt Technicians during the period from December, 1954 to October, 1956. Washington, D.C.: United States Department of State, 1957. Pp. 32.

642. "A Survey of Fulbright Alumni Groups," *Institute of International Education: News Bulletin*, XXXIV (April, 1959), 35-42.

643. *Survey Report of Returned Participants*. Athens, Greece: Training Division, United States AID Mission to Greece, Agency for International Development, United States Department of State, 1963. Pp. 231.

Chiefly tables.

644. United States High Commissioner for Germany, Office of Public Affairs, Bonn, Germany. *Dissemination Record of Exchangee Categories for*

Significant Areas of American Life. Washington, D.C.: Bureau of Educational and Cultural Affairs, United States Department of State, 1954. Pp. 128.

645. _____. West German Receptivity and Reactions to the Exchange of Persons Program. Washington, D.C.: Bureau of Educational and Cultural Affairs, United States Department of State, 1952. Pp. 112.

646. United States Operations Mission to Indonesia. An Evaluation of the Participant Training Program in Indonesia. Djakarta, Indonesia: State Printing Office, 1959. Pp. 165.

Presents results of nation-wide survey made by the United States International Cooperation Administration and the Interdepartmental Coordinating Committee of the Indonesian Government.

*647. Useem, John and Ruth H. The Western-Educated Man in India; A Study of His Social Roles and Influence. New York: Dryden Press, 1955. Pp. 237.

The subject is the consequences of Western education; data were gathered from interviews with over one hundred Indians who had studied in Great Britain and the United States. Topics for discussions include (a) attitudes of students prior to going abroad, (b) changed attitude and outlook as a result of foreign study, (c) diffusion of knowledge and technique upon return, (d) implications for international understanding as a result of foreign study, and (e) practical suggestions for the improvement of student exchange programs. The authors make a special appeal for more adequate academic orientation to the new environment and more attention to the students' prospective use of their education upon return.

648. Warmbrunn, Werner. Observations of Education and International Exchange in Asia. New York: National Association for Foreign Student Affairs, 1961.

649. White, Aurilla. Annexes to Guidelines for

Evaluating the Participant Training Program. (See No. 854.)

650. _____. Survey Guidelines for Evaluation of Participant Training Programs. (See No. 855.)

651. Woodrow Wilson School of Public and International Affairs. Cultural Contacts Project. 3 vols. Washington, D.C.: Bureau of Educational and Cultural Affairs, United States Department of State, 1951.

    Vol. I.   An Evaluation of the Longtime Effects of Educational Exchange in Belgium. Pp. 208.
    Vol. II. Opinions Belges. Pp. 219.
    Vol. III. Summary and Conclusions. Pp. 67.

PART VI

INSTITUTIONAL RELATIONSHIPS
IN INTERNATIONAL EDUCATION

IV

CHAPTER 14 UNITED STATES GOVERNMENT POLICY

652. AID Participant Training Program--How It Works. Washington, D.C.: International Training Division, Agency for International Development, United States Department of State, 1963. Pp. 8.

653. Adams, Walter. A Report on the Strategic Importance of Western Europe. Washington, D.C.: Government Printing Office, 1964. Pp. 18.

   The Acting Chairman, United States Advisory Commission on International Educational and Cultural Affairs, notes the neglect of Western Europe in international education policies of the United States.

654. African Students and Study Programs in the United States: Report, August 15, 1965, and Hearings, June 15-23, 1965, Pursuant to H. Res. 84. Before the Subcommittee on Africa, Committee on Foreign Affairs, United States House of Representatives. (89th Cong., 1st sess.) Washington, D.C.: Government Printing Office, 1965. Pp. 169.

655. Annual Summary of Foreign Agricultural Training. Washington, D.C.: Foreign Agricultural Service, United States Department of Agriculture, annually.

*656. A Beacon of Hope: The Exchange-of-Persons Program. (0-683580.) Washington, D.C.: Advisory Commission on International Educational and Cultural Affairs, United States Department of State, 1963. Pp. 65.

   The educational and cultural exchange program of the United States Department of State is fully reviewed. The focus is on the foreign grantee although American grantees are discussed in relation to professors and lecturers. An impressive array of investigation methods is used: (a) interviews with foreign grantees of twenty countries, (b) an inquiry of United States embassies, (c) personal research by Commission members, (d) interviews with high ranking officials in Washington, and (e) a review of research over the past decade. Thus, a study "in depth" emerges. Not only is the present program evaluated, but many recommendations are offered, including those concerning government and university cooperation.

*657. Behavioral Sciences and the National Security. Report No. 4 with Part IX of Winning the Cold War: The U.S. Ideological Offensive. Hearings before the Subcommittee on International Organizations and Movements, Committee on Foreign Affairs, United States House of Representatives. (89th Cong., 1st sess.) Washington, D.C.: Government Printing Office, 1965. Pp. 202.

The proceedings of Congressional hearings held following the publicity on the Department of the Army's Project Camelot, which dealt with social change in developing countries. A brief Committee summary statement with recommendations precedes testimony, including that of Secretary of State Dean Rusk.

*658. Blum, Robert, and the American Assembly (eds.). Cultural Affairs and Foreign Relations. Englewood Cliffs, N.J.: Prentice-Hall, Inc., 1963. Pp. 184.

Five essays sponsored by the American Assembly: "The Nature and Development of United States Cultural Relations," George N. Shuster; "The Role of the Arts and the Humanities," W. McNeil Lowry and Gertrude S. Hooker; "Education, Foreign Policy, and International Relations," Howard E. Wilson; "International Cooperation and the Two Faces of Science," Roger Revelle; "The Past and Future in Perspective," Philip H. Coombs. The volume concludes with the final report of the 22nd American Assembly, which presents twenty concise recommendations for policy improvement.

659. Bureau of Social Science Research, Inc. *The Educational Exchange Program: An Appraisal by 193 Educators and 77 Organization and Business Executives*. Washington, D.C.: Bureau of Educational and Cultural Affairs, United States Department of State, 1953.

660. Cohen, Herman J. "Fulbright Program in Latin America," *Institute of International Education: News Bulletin*, XXXV (April, 1960), 8-17.

661. *Contract Program in Research and Analysis*. Washington, D.C.: Agency for International Development, United States Department of State, 1964. Pp. 18.

*662. Coombs, Philip H. *The Fourth Dimension of Foreign Policy: Educational and Cultural Affairs*. New York: Published for the Council on Foreign Relations by Harper & Row, 1964. Pp. 158.

In a reassessment of the "educational component" of United States foreign policy by the first Assistant Secretary of State for Educational and Cultural Affairs, the author tries to answer these basic questions: (a) What do we mean by "educational and cultural" affairs and how did they become an important part of United States foreign policy? (b) How did the policies, programs, and issues of today's policies develop? (c) What is going on in the field today, and who is doing it? (d) What are other nations doing and what can we learn from their experience? (e) What are the achievements and failures of our policy? (f) What should be done in the future, and what role should government play?

663. Cotner, Thomas E. "The Role of the U.S. Federal Government in International Education: The Office of Education," *Education for National Development, Focus: Latin America*. 6th Annual Conference on International Understanding, American Association of Colleges for Teacher Education, University of Pittsburgh, April 16-18, 1964, pp. 39-46. (Out of print.)

664. _____. A Summary of the Exchange and Training Programs, Office of Education, United States Department of Health, Education, and Welfare, 1939-1966. Washington, D.C.: Office of Education, the Department, 1966.

Besides a brief historical summary, statistics are included on the International Teacher Development Program, the Leader Program, and the Teacher Exchange Program.

665. Cultural Presentations Program of the U.S. Department of State, July 1, 1963-June 30, 1964. ("Department of State Publication," No. 7819, "International Information and Cultural Series," No. 88.) Washington, D.C.: Bureau of Educational and Cultural Affairs, the Department, 1965. Pp. 105.

The impact of the performing groups is described, recommendations of the Advisory Committee on the Arts for program improvement are presented, and the 1962 Larsen-Wolfe Report is reprinted with its examination of all phases of the State Department's Educational and Cultural Programs.

666. Donovan, James A., Jr. "The Foreign Leader Program of the Department of State: One View," Educational Record, XXXIV (October, 1953), 327-35.

*667. "Education as an Instrument of National Goals," Phi Delta Kappan, XLVII (December, 1965), entire issue.

The following essays are included: "The National Commitment to Education," Francis Keppel; "Education and the Wealth of Nations," Don Adams; "National Goals and International Values," Harold Taylor; "Educational Planning in the Context of National Social Policy," C. Arnold Anderson; "Problems in Administration and Finance When National Goals Become Primary," H. Thomas James; "The Successes and Failures of AID," Harold L. Enarson; "A Case for Polycultural Education," Oliver J. Caldwell; "Investment in Education and Economic Development," Nicholas DeWitt; "Education for Economic Development in India and Pakistan," Willis P. Porter; "Notes on Education Behind the Iron Curtain," John S. Brubacher; "Is South America Making Progress?," Joseph S. Roucek; "International Education: Its Claims on Ingenuity," Gordon I. Swanson; "Teaching Materials for Foreign Area Instruction," Robert F. Byrnes; "Teacher Education for International Goals," H. Kenneth Barker.

*668. Educational and Cultural Diplomacy. ("International and Cultural Series.") Washington, D.C.: United States Department of State, annually.

This summary presents extensive statistical information on exchange of persons and a description of United States government activity in international education during that year.

669. "The Effectiveness of the Educational and Cultural Exchange Program of the United States Department of State," Excerpts from the Report to Congress, Higher Education, XIX (July, 1963), 26-28.

670. "The Effectiveness of the Educational and Cultural Exchange Program of the U.S. Department of State," Overseas, II (April, 1963), 22-25.

*671. Elder, Robert Ellsworth. The Foreign Leader Program: Operations in the United States. Washington, D.C.: Brookings Institution, 1961. Pp. 115.

The thorough study was made at the request of the United States Department of State to "describe, analyze, and appraise the Foreign Leader Program, particularly to assess its present effectiveness and to suggest possibilities for improvement, both immediate and long-term." The program itself is designed to develop in other countries a core of individuals who are able to relay a fair assessment of the United States and its people. The participants selected for short travel tours of the United States include only those presently occupying leadership positions in their own country.

672. Experiment in International Understanding: A Report with a Close-Up of the U.S. Educational Exchange Program with Italy. Washington, D.C.: Board of Foreign Scholarships, Bureau of Educational and Cultural Affairs, United States Department of State, 1963. Pp. 76.

673. <u>Foreign Visitor Programs: Foreign Leader Program, Foreign Specialist Program, Educational Travel Program, Volunteer Visitor Program.</u> ("Department of State Publication," No. 7631; "International Information and Cultural Series," No. 86.) Washington, D.C.: Bureau of Educational and Cultural Affairs, The Department, 1964. Pp. 11.

*674. Frankel, Charles. <u>The Neglected Aspect of Foreign Affairs; American Educational and Cultural Policy Abroad.</u> Washington, D.C.: The Brookings Institution, 1965. Pp. 156.

This important study was completed just prior to the author's appointment as Assistant Secretary of State for Educational and Cultural Affairs. The author examines the governing purposes, institutional arrangements, and current practices in United States educational and cultural policy. Three basic reforms are suggested. (a) "Educational and cultural affairs need to be raised to a level of authority consonant with their significance for the relations of the American people with other nations." (b) "The setting within which educational and cultural policy is formed and implemented needs to be changed." (c) "A new, more cooperative, and more binding relationship needs to be formed between government and the private educational and cultural communities." Several explicit recommendations, including the creation of a semi-autonomous foundation for educational and cultural exchange, are offered.

*675. Fraser, Stewart (ed.). <u>Governmental Policy and International Education.</u> New York: John Wiley & Sons, Inc., 1965. Pp. 373.

Sixteen papers from a symposium at the International Center, George Peabody College for Teachers, Nashville, Tennessee, October 22-24, 1964. This volume is a pioneering effort to compare a variety of government policies on student exchange: "The United Nations and International Relations," Adlai E. Stevenson; "Criteria for Judging the Worth of an International Educational Program," Harold R. W. Benjamin; "Historical Development of Governmental Interest in International Higher Education," William W. Brickman; "The Cultural

Background of International Education," Ina Corinne Brown; "Education Comes of Age Around the World," Oliver J. Caldwell; "The Program of the Comparative Education Center, University of Chicago," C. Arnold Anderson; "The Development of the National Association for Foreign Student Affairs from 'Idea to Institution'," M. R. B. Klinger; "Governmental Encouragement and Control of International Education in Communist China," Theodore H. E. Chen; "The Experience of Foreign Students in China," René Goldman; "Foreign Students in the Soviet Union and East European Countries," Josef A. Mestenhauser; "Sino-Soviet Educational Cooperation: 1950-60," Stewart E. Fraser; "Governmental Policy and International Education: United States of America," James M. Davis; "Governmental Policy and International Education: Canada," Joseph Katz; "Foreign Student Exchanges: France," Jacques Poujol; "Foreign Student Exchanges: Germany," Weigand Pabsch; "Modernization as Affected by Governmental and International Educational Influences: Japan," Donald K. Adams and Robert Bjork; "Governmental Policy and International Education: A Selected and Partially Annotated Bibliography," Franklin Parker.

676. Goodwin, Leonard. <u>American Professors in Asia: A Study of the Selection and Adaptation of Fifty American Professors Who Went to India, Pakistan, and Korea Under the Fulbright-Hays Program During 1962-63</u>. (See No. 355.)

*677. Haviland, H. Field, Jr. "Federal Programs of International Education" in <u>Higher Education and the Federal Government</u>. Ed. Charles G. Dobbins. Washington, D.C.: American Council on Education, 1963, pp. 76-88.

The agencies of government involved in international education and a description of their activities is followed by a discussion of three policy issues associated with these programs: (a) basic goals of universities and departments concerned, (b) development assistance which is acquiring the greatest proportion of Federal backing for international education, (c) United States scholar export via the Fulbright-Hays Act. The author urges universities to assess their resources immediately and think in terms of long-range institution and government goals.

678. Hearings on the Foreign Assistance Act of 1963. Hearings before the Committee on Foreign Relations, United States House of Representatives. (88th Cong., 1st sess.; on H. R. 5490, Part I.) Washington, D.C.: Government Printing Office, 1963.

Secretary of Defense Robert S. McNamara testifies on the military training of foreign participants, pp. 53-64.

679. Hearings on the Foreign Assistance Act of 1963. Hearings before the Committee on Foreign Relations, United States Senate. (88th Cong., 1st sess.) Washington, D.C.: Government Printing Office, 1963.

Secretary of Defense Robert S. McNamara testifies on the military training of foreign participants, pp. 165-79.

680. Hubbert, Erin. "Evaluation of the Fulbright Program," Institute of International Education: News Bulletin, XXXV (April, 1960), 39-45.

681. International Education Program, 1966. New York: Education and World Affairs, 1966.

The text of the draft, International Education Act of 1966, an appraisal of it, and President Johnson's speeches about it are included.

682. International Educational, Cultural and Related Activities for African Countries South of the Sahara. (See No. 837.)

683. International Research Associates, Inc. The Effectiveness of the Exchange Program: A Study in Twenty Countries in All Regions of the World. 2 vols. Washington, D.C.: United States Department of State, 1962.
    Vol. I. Pp. 162.
    Vol. II. Pp. 200.

An extensive survey of 3,842 grantees and administrators of the program in several countries. While the goal of mutual understanding was generally reached, replies included considerable criticism of our economic, political, and educational systems, particularly by exchangees from Western Europe. The study was part of the data analyzed for the Beacon of Hope report of the Advisory Commission on International Educational and Cultural Affairs. (See No. 656.)

684. International Teacher Development Program. (OE-14003-date.) Annual Report to the Bureau of Educational and Cultural Affairs, United States Department of State. Washington, D.C.: Office of Education, United States Department of Health, Education and Welfare, annually.

*685. Johnson, Walter, and Colligan, Francis J. The Fulbright Program: A History. With a foreword by J. W. Fulbright. Chicago: University of Chicago Press, 1965. Pp. 380.

An extremely thorough description and analysis of the Fulbright Program from its inception in 1946 to the present. The program is discussed in relation to several individual countries and its general future direction is assessed. An excellent bibliographical essay concludes the volume.

*686. Laves, Walter H. C. Toward a National Effort in International and Cultural Affairs. (87th Cong., 1st sess., House Committee on Foreign Affairs, Doc. No. 199.) Washington, D.C.: Government Printing Office, 1961. Also, in slightly abbreviated form, a pamphlet in the "Department of State Publication," No. 7238, "International Information and Cultural Series," No. 78, 1961. Pp. 82.

This report to the United States Advisory Commission on Educational Exchange thoroughly analyzes the goals and means required for an effective United States policy in international cultural affairs. The report begins with a warning:

> Although the United States has probably contributed more than any other nation to postwar educational and cultural programs and has shown more consistent commitment than others, the magnitude of the task is such that this considerable effort has been wholly inadequate.

After discussing the international setting for United States policies, the author explores five types of government programs--programs designed (a) to advance knowledge and strengthen the world community of education, science, and culture; (b) to develop understanding abroad of United States culture and institutions; (c) to increase understanding of foreign cultures and institutions among Americans; (d) to meet the educational, scientific, and cultural needs of newly developing countries; and (e) to encourage the development of societies in which democratic institutions can develop. Particular emphasis is placed on the problem of coordinating both government and private agencies engaged in these tasks.

687. McNamara, Robert S. "An Information Program for Foreign Military Trainees and Visitors in the United States." Memorandum for Army, Navy, Air Force, ISA,M, and Commanders of Unified and Specified Commands. Mimeo., United States Department of Defense, September 13, 1963.

This memorandum marks the beginning of a program to include nonmilitary education for foreign military students.

688. Military Assistance Training Programs of the U.S. Government. (See No. 416.)

689. "A New Basis for Technical Assistance Through Colleges and Universities," Congressional Record. (89th Cong., 1st sess.) CXI (February 19, 1965), 3,120-24.

Senator George McGovern explains his proposal (Bill S.1212) to authorize federal monies for the establishment and maintenance of development centers at several colleges and universities which will undertake technical assistance projects. He argues that federal aid is necessary in order to ease the financial burden upon the institutions of higher education, and also to allow maximum performance of available personnel as a result of careful and long-range planning. The text of the bill is included.

690. Peace Corps. Annual Report to Congress. Washington, D.C.: Government Printing Office, annually.

UNITED STATES GOVERNMENT POLICY

691. Pierson, Constance L., and O'Grady, Lorraine. U.S. Government Exchange and Training Programs for Foreign Women. ("Policy Research Study.") Washington, D.C.: External Research Staff, Bureau of Intelligence and Research, United States Department of State, 1963. Pp. 51.

692. Public Laws.

   Of the many laws governing United States government activity in international education, the following are especially important: Public Law 584, 79th Congress, the Fulbright Act; Public Law 256, 87th Congress, the Mutual Educational and Cultural Exchange Act of 1961 (the Fulbright-Hays Act); Public Law 864, 85th Congress, the National Defense Education Act of 1958.

693. Quattlebaum, Charles A. "Government Programs in International Education," Educational Record, XL (July, 1959), 249-55.

694. Report of a Task Force on "Exchange of Persons," by an ad hoc task force appointed by Pres.-elect Kennedy, January 5, 1961.

   James M. Davis was chairman of the task force.

695. Rosenzweig, Robert M. "Foreign Policy and Education: A Confusion of Purposes," Journal of Higher Education, XXXVII (May, 1966), 277-80.

   A review of Johnson's and Colligan's The Fulbright Program: A History. (See No. 685.)

696. The Scope and Distribution of U.S. Military and Economic Assistance Programs. Report to the President of the United States from the Committee to Strengthen the Security of the Free World. (S1.2:AS7.) Washington, D.C.: Government Printing Office, 1963. Pp. 25.

   Lucius Clay was chairman of the committee.

697. Semiannual Report to the Board of Foreign Scholarships, January 1 to June 30, 1964. Prepared by the Institute of International

Education. Washington, D.C.: Government Printing Office, 1964. Pp. 10. Suppl., <u>Statistics on U.S. Graduate Student Grants Under the Fulbright-Hays Program, 1964-65</u>. 1964. Pp. 21.

698. <u>Sequel to a Beacon of Hope, the Exchange-of-Persons Program; A Report</u>. Washington, D.C.: Advisory Commission on International Educational and Cultural Affairs, United States Department of State, 1964. Pp. 34.

The second annual report of the Commission includes a progress report on the recommendations of <u>A Beacon of Hope</u> (see No. 656) which remains the most thorough analysis of the Government's Exchange of Persons program.

699. Sinauer, Ernst M. <u>Training of Foreign Nationals in the United States by the Department of Defense: The Role of Communication</u>. ("Air Force Report.") Prepared with the assistance of the Behavioral Sciences Division, Air Force Office of Scientific Research. Washington, D.C.: United States Department of Defense, 1964. Pp. 57.

700. "Sino-Soviet Bloc Exchanges with the Free World in 1960," ("Intelligence Report," No. 8401, United States Bureau of Intelligence and Research) in Hearings on S.1154, the <u>Mutual Educational and Cultural Exchange</u> Act. Hearings before the Committee on Foreign Relations, United States Senate, April 27, 1961. (87th Cong., 1st sess.) Washington, D.C.: Government Printing Office, 1961, pp. 165-209.

701. <u>A Summary Report on the United States Exchange Program with the Soviet Union</u>. Washington, D.C.: Soviet and Eastern European Exchanges Staff, Bureau of European Affairs, United States Department of State, 1964. Pp. 11.

A short summary of the program from 1958 to 1963.

702. <u>Teacher and Scholar Abroad: First-Person Reports of the U.S. Exchange Program</u>. (See No. 280.)

703. Technical Assistance Training Program in Education. (OE-14046-63.) Report covering fiscal years 1961-63. Washington, D.C.: Office of Education, United States Department of Health, Education and Welfare, 1965.

   Discusses training activities by the country involved and assesses the effectiveness of the program. Lengthy statistical tables are included.

*704. Thomson, Charles A., and Laves, Walter H. C. Cultural Relations and U.S. Foreign Policy. Bloomington: Indiana University Press, 1963. Pp. 227.

   The authors analyze the recent history of United States government cultural relations and suggest explicit guidelines for future policy. A bibliography is included.

705. Training for Development; AID Participant Training for Social and Economic Development of Cooperating Countries. 3rd ed. Washington, D.C.: Agency for International Development, United States Department of State, 1963.

   The explanation of the program includes quantitative data tables.

706. Training for Leadership and Service. Proceedings of the National Conference on the International Training Programs of the Agency for International Development, June 25-26, 1962. Washington, D.C.: International Training Division, The Agency, United States Department of State, 1962. Pp. 88.

707. Training of Foreign Nationals Under MAP. Annex E, Composite Report of the President's Committee to Study the United States Military Assistance Program. Washington, D.C.: United States Department of Defense, 1959.

708. Training of Foreign Personnel by the U.S. Army. (Change I, AR 551-50.) Washington, D.C.: United States Department of Defense, 1964.

709. <u>Twenty Years of United States Government Programs in Cultural Relations</u>. (See No. 297.)

710. <u>A Two-Way Street: Benefits Accruing from the International Training Programs of AID</u>. Washington, D.C.: International Training Division, Agency for International Development, United States Department of State, 1963. Pp. 48.

711. United States Department of State. "Educational and Cultural Exchange with Africa: The Program of the Department of State," <u>African Studies Bulletin</u>, IV (May, 1961), 1-8.

*712. <u>The U.S. Office of Education: A New International Dimension</u>. A Report to the U.S. Commissioner of Education. New York: Education and World Affairs, 1964. Pp. 72.

The international aspects of the Office of Education are assessed and related to its domestic responsibilities. The report proposes new and expanded activities. Analyses and recommendations are made under the following topics: (a) the development of the office, (b) organization and present international functions of the office, (c) the future international role of the office, (d) implementation of the role of the office and relations with various agencies, and (e) staffing and organization of the office. Herman B Wells was chairman of the committee which prepared the report.

713. <u>Winning the Cold War: The U.S. Ideological Offensive</u>. Hearings before the Subcommittee on International Organizations and Movements, Committee on Foreign Affairs, United States House of Representatives. (88th Cong., 1st and 2nd sess.) Washington, D.C.: Government Printing Office.
    Part IV. <u>U.S. Cultural and Artistic Exchanges; U.S. Student and Leader Exchanges</u>. 1963.
    Part VII. <u>U.S. Government Agencies and Programs, Agency for International Development and the Department of Defense</u>. 1964.

714. Young, Francis A. "The Conference Board of Associated Research Councils in the United States: A Brief Historical Account with Special Reference to National and International Manpower Problems," *Social Sciences Information* (International Social Science Council), IV (June, 1965), 111-27.

CHAPTER 15 — HIGHER EDUCATION AND THE UNITED STATES GOVERNMENT

The relationships here designate the process, organization, and agreements whereby the Government contracts with institutions of higher education for the use of personnel for teaching, advising, or other service abroad in government-sponsored international programs.

715. AID-Financed University Contracts. Washington, D.C.: Contract Services Division, Agency for International Development, United States Department of State, quarterly.

716. "AID-University Relationships," (SRI Project No. 4634.), Report of a meeting at Stanford Research Institute, Menlo Park, September 20, 1963, sponsored by Education and World Affairs. Mimeo., Education and World Affairs, 1963. Pp. 23.

*717. Baumgartner, Leona. "The National Commitment to Developing Nations and the Universities," Remarks to the American Council on Education, Washington, D.C., October 2-4, 1963. Available from Education and World Affairs, Inc.

The former Assistant Administrator of the Agency for International Development asks for (a) a realization that education is an investment in human capital formation, (b) a recognition of the central role of strong governments in the process of educational development, (c) more careful evaluation of educational expenditures, and (d) a thorough re-thinking of AID-university relationships and methods.

*718. Bell, David E. The University Contribution to the Developing Nations. (Press Release No. AID-63-217.) Address delivered at the regional Conference of Education and World Affairs, East Lansing, Michigan, October 11, 1963. Washington, D.C.: United States Department of State, 1963. Pp. 19.

The Administrator of the Agency for International Development discusses several questions concerning university-government relationships in international development, including fuller university involvement and commitment; more coordination of government and university recruitment, training and career development for international service; and a new emphasis on evaluation in every project.

719. Blueprints and Experience. Addresses and Summary of Proceedings, 1957 Annual Conference on University Contracts Abroad. Washington, D.C.: American Council on Education, 1958.

*720. Caldwell, Lynton K. "The Universities and International Technical Assistance," Journal of Higher Education, XXXVI (May, 1965), 266-73.

The difference between theory and practice in university execution of government contracts is due to decentralized university administration, lack of university rewards (namely research) in the contract program, and the inability of many universities to plan ahead. For the government to obtain maximum university commitment to contract programs, the relationship must be based on the following:

> (1) Universities cannot risk full commitment to contract programs for which government financial and logistical support is subject to abrupt, unpredictable, and arbitrary change. (2) The duration of a program . . . should be for a period sufficient to accomplish program objectives. (3) Within the general terms of the contract, the university should be accorded a high degree of operational flexibility and of discretion in making the best use of its resources. (4) There should be a research-and-development component in every major government-university technical-assistance contract for the purpose of cumulatively enriching national resources for international technical assistance.

*721. Gardner, John W. **A.I.D. and the Universities**. New York: Education and World Affairs, Inc., and Agency for International Development, 1964. Pp. 57. (Out of print.)

This report to the Administrator of the Agency for International Development is a major reassessment of the AID-university relationship, full of recommendations for better use of our resources. The universities should commit their resources more fully to contract responsibilities undertaken and government agencies should accept universities more completely into senior partnership. Universities must "recognize such activity as an integral part of university life and work"; an eight-point criterion is suggested for the selection of universities to operate overseas contracts. The problems of participant training are also acknowledged and the report notes that trainees often receive training not relevant to their needs. "The importance of specially tailored programs and their high cost should be frankly acknowledged if this shortcoming is to be remedied." Research on development is another area in which both AID and universities need to share responsibilities. The report concludes with several important suggestions and comments on AID organization. A bibliography is included.

722. Hughes, Thomas L. "Scholars and Foreign Policy: Varieties of Research Experience," **Department of State Bulletin**, LIII (November 8, 1965), 747-58.

723. Humphrey, Richard A. (ed.). **Toward a Foreign Policy for Higher Education**. Addresses and Summary of Proceedings of the 5th Annual Conference on University Contracts Abroad. Washington, D.C.: American Council on Education, 1960. Pp. 114.

Representatives of major educational institutions and top government officials emphasize the necessary cooperation between government and university in order to meet the common goals of each.

724. _____ (ed.). **University Projects Abroad**. Papers presented at the Conference on

University Contracts Abroad, Michigan State University, East Lansing, Nov. 17-18, 1955. Washington, D.C.: American Council on Education, 1956. Pp. 66.

725. Little, J. Kenneth. A Survey of Federal Programs in Higher Education: Final Report. (OE-50034; Bulletin 1963, No. 6.) Washington, D.C.: Government Printing Office, 1962.

726. Mildenberger, Kenneth W. "The Federal Government and the Universities" in "The Non-Western World in Higher Education." (See No 95.)

727. Report to the President on Government Contracting for Research and Development. (87th Cong., 2nd sess.; Sen. Doc. No. 94.) Prepared by the Bureau of the Budget and referred to the Committee on Government Operations, United States Senate. Washington, D.C.: Government Printing Office, 1962. Pp. 68.

728. The Role of American Higher Education in Relation to Developing Areas. (See No. 783.)

*729. Rosenzweig, Robert M. "Universities and the Foreign Assistance Program," Journal of Higher Education, XXXV (October, 1964), 359-66.

The author pleads for a government-university relationship that is consistent with the central tasks of education.

730. The Scholar and the Policy Maker. A Series of Talks Given at the Plenary Session of the Association for Asian Studies, Washington, D.C.: March 20, 1964. ("External Research Paper," No. 151.) Washington, D.C.: External Research Staff, Bureau of Intelligence and Research, United States Department of State, 1964. Pp. 23.

Discusses the proper relationship between the scholar and policy-maker--what kind of cross-fertilization is desirable? The speakers are Roger Hilsman, George E. Taylor, Charles Wolf, Jr., and Henry S. Rowen, with Robert Blum as chairman.

*731. Shiver, Elizabeth N. (ed.). Education and

the Modernizing of Nations. Summary proceedings, Conference sponsored by the Commission on International Education of the American Council on Education and Wayne State University, September, 1964. Washington, D.C.: American Council on Education, 1965. Pp. 66.

The Conference was organized with two purposes in view:

> (1) to provide a forum for review of the government-university partnership in overseas development, and (2) to provide a place in the dialogue for the concerns of industry and labor, whose growing commitments abroad presuppose dependence upon higher education in many ways.

Three principal addresses are included: "Education and the Modernizing of Nations," David E. Bell; "Business, Labor, and the Universities in the Modernizing of Nations," John W. McConnell; "Developing Higher Education in the Newly Developing Countries," Frederick Harbison. Summaries of the working sessions conclude the volume.

732. Silvert, Kalman H. "American Academic Ethics and Social Research Abroad: The Lesson of Project Camelot," American Universities Field Staff Reports Service. ("West Coast South America Series," XII,3.) 1965.

733. Special Committee to Study the Foreign Aid Program, Committee on Foreign Relations, United States Senate. The Use of Private Contractors in Foreign Aid Programs. (85th Cong., 1st sess.; Committee Print.) Prepared by Jerome Jacobson Associates. Washington, D.C.: Government Printing Office, 1957. Pp. 101.

734. Wells, Herman B "Widening Horizons," Educational Record, XXXVIII (April, 1957), 136-40

The author discusses the "widening horizons" of our colleges and universities in terms of the opportunities and obligations of overseas contract programs.

CHAPTER 16 — HIGHER EDUCATION AND INTERNATIONAL ORGANIZATIONS

735. Asher, Robert E., et al. The United Nations and Economic and Social Co-operation. Washington, D.C.: Brookings Institution, 1958.

736. Cerych, Ladislav. Problems of Aid to Education in Developing Countries. (See No. 756.)

737. Enarson, Harold L. "University Education in Central America," Journal of Higher Education, XXXIV (April, 1963), 196-204.

    This article summarizes the present capacities of CSUCA (Higher Council of Central American Universities) and its importance in the future growth of Central American university education--an education which is in need of drastic reforms. Problems include: lack of central direction within the universities themselves, resulting inefficiency, part-time teachers and students, rigid curriculum with few electives, and political involvement. CSUCA is trying to designate certain universities to specialize in certain fields for the entire region, set region-wide standards, and inaugurate systematic exchange programs. Meanwhile, the spirit of university cooperation has risen and funds from governments and foundations have increased.

738. Holland, Kenneth. "A Catalyst for Inter-American Higher Education," Teachers College Record, LXIV (May, 1963), 687-92.

*739. Laves, Walter H. C., and Thomson, Charles A. UNESCO: Purpose, Progress, Prospects. Bloomington: Indiana University Press, 1957. Pp. 469.

    An extremely thorough study of the ideas and activities that have become UNESCO. "The book tries to explain for the general reader what UNESCO has done and why, and to the extent that judgment may be possible, how useful UNESCO has been." The volume is less a general history of the organization and more "an explanation and analysis of its program." The discussion covers pre-UNESCO institutions and activities, issues facing those who drafted the Constitution, and stages of program development. Bibliographical references are included in the "Notes."

740. Lawson, Edwin D. "Why Not U.N. Regional Universities?," Journal of Higher Education, XXXIV (November, 1965), 449-52.

741. Marin, Juan. "The Organization of American States and Education," Teachers College Record, LXV (October, 1963), 11-16.

742. Parker, Franklin. "UNESCO in Perspective," International Review of Education, X (1964), 326-31.

743. Sathyamurthy, T. V. "Changing Concepts of Intellectual Co-operation," International Review of Education, IX,4 (1963-64), 385-95.

A review of intellectual cooperation via the League of Nations and UNESCO. The author concludes saying that the

> . . . secretariat of UNESCO under the direction of the Director-General would do well to consider itself as not merely the policy-executing agency of the member states, but also as a custodian of some universal goals to which UNESCO is committed.

744. _____. The Politics of International Cooperation; Contrasting Conceptions of UNESCO. Geneva, Switzerland, Librairie Droz, 1964. Pp. 314.

745. Shuster, George N. UNESCO: Assessment and Promise. 1st ed. New York: Published for the Council on Foreign Relations by Harper & Row, 1963. Pp. 130.

A bibliography is included.

CHAPTER 17 — HIGHER EDUCATION AND INTERNATIONAL DEVELOPMENT

The focus in this section is on technical assistance in developing areas. Several entries that are concerned solely with the factors of education in national development are included because United States universities working abroad are often as much concerned with these elements as are the local institutions. No effort has been made to include the many often valuable and revealing periodic reports on specific university contract operations abroad.

746. Adams, Don. "Education and the Wealth of Nations." (See No. 667.)

747. Adams, Richard N., and Cumberland, Charles C. United States University Cooperation in Latin America. A Study Based on Selected Programs in Bolivia, Chile, Peru, and Mexico. East Lansing: Institute of Research on Overseas Programs, Michigan State University, 1960. Pp. 264.

The authors have not written an evaluation but a review of the general impact and the kinds of activities and problems involved. Contents include thirteen case studies with discussions of origins, contract and financial information, and objectives. The remainder of the book discusses general project experience on a comparative basis.

748. Adams, Walter, and Garraty, John A. Is the World Our Campus? East Lansing: Michigan State University Press, 1960. Pp. 180.

A vivid, even sensational, account of overseas programs of American universities. The authors discover

> . . . that not all foreign assistance is worthy of the nation's private or public purse; that not all American universities (regardless of their prestige at home) are responsible purveyors of technical assistance; that many (perhaps most) professors engaged in overseas projects are far from ideal ambassadors; and that the university-administered and ICA- or foundation-financed contracts are not necessarily effective instruments for helping other countries.

749. Anderson, C. Arnold. "Educational Planning in the Context of National Social Policy." (See No. 667.)

750. Andrus, J. Russell. "Technical Assistance Through Inter-University Contracts," Higher Education, XII (January, 1956), 75-80.

751. Baumgartner, Leona. "The National Commitment to Developing Nations and the Universities." (See No. 717.)

752. Bigelow, Karl W. "Afro-Anglo-American Program for Teacher Education in Africa," Institute of International Education: News Bulletin, XXXVI (November, 1960), 41-46.

The program includes the Columbia and London schools of education plus several African universities and is financed by a Carnegie grant. The prime objective is to assist African institutions through the cooperation of British and American resources. The author describes the complicated system of student-faculty exchanges and a training course for Americans planning to do educational work in Africa.

753. Bronfenbrenner, Martin. Academic Encounter; The American University in Japan and Korea. New York: Free Press of Glencoe, 1961. Pp. 260.

This study of eighteen American university affiliations with Japanese and Korean institutions was made in 1958. Numerous suggestions and recommendations conclude the volume.

*754. Butts, R. Freeman. *American Education in International Development*. 1st ed. New York: Harper & Row, 1963. Pp. 138.

The author discusses what he considers to be the three main stages of America's educational affiliations with other countries since World War II: (a) the continuing process of informing ourselves and others about each other via standard formal course work and educational exchanges, (b) the providing of technical assistance to governments and educational institutions abroad, (c) our government's response to requests for American teachers to become regular instructors in schools and universities abroad. A preliminary evaluation of the Peace Corps is included, and a final chapter dwells on the problems facing both those receiving and those offering educational aid. The volume's special importance lies in its recognition of the complex political, social, and economic problems countries face in trying to strengthen their educational systems.

755. Caldwell, Oliver J. "Africa and American Education," *American Association of Colleges for Teacher Education Yearbook: 1961*. 14th Yearbook, Annual Meeting, Chicago, 1961, pp. 75-82.

756. Cerych, Ladislav. *Problems of Aid to Education in Developing Countries*. ("Praeger Special Studies in International Economics and Development.") New York: Published for the Atlantic Institute by Frederick A. Praeger, Publishers, 1965. Pp. 226.

The author suggests some of the basic features of a consistent policy of external aid to education and discusses how such a policy might be coordinated internationally. A bibliography is included.

757. Coleman, James S. (ed.). *Education and Political Development*. Princeton, N.J.: Princeton University Press, 1965. Pp. 620.

758. Cormack, Margaret L., et al. *The International Programs of American Universities*. (See No. 822.)

759. Cotner, Thomas E. "Teacher Education and U.S. Training Programs with African Countries," <u>American Association of Colleges for Teacher Education Yearbook: 1962.</u> 15th Yearbook, Annual Meeting, Chicago, 1962, pp. 78-83.

760. Curle, Adam. <u>Educational Strategy for Developing Societies; A Study of Educational and Social Factors in Relation to Economic Growth.</u> London: Tavistock Publications, 1963. Pp. 180.

   A bibliography is included.

761. <u>Design for Pakistan.</u> A Report on Assistance to the Pakistan Planning Commission by the Ford Foundation and Harvard University. New York: Ford Foundation, 1965. Pp. 39.

   This pamphlet relates the Foundation's and Harvard University's involvement in a successful ten-year program to create a competent technical planning body for Pakistan. Among several problems discussed are the necessity for concern with certain aspects of operationalizing carefully drawn plans, alternative plans for overseas training, adviser qualifications, the advisory and decision-making roles of the outsider, and the long-range nature of the project itself.

762. DeWitt, Nicholas. "Investment in Education and Economic Development." (See No. 667.)

763. "Educational Exchange for the Mutual Development of Nations." (See No. 266.)

764. <u>Educational Exchange in the Economic Development of Nations.</u> (See No. 389.)

765. <u>Educational Investment in the Pacific Community.</u> 5th Annual Conference Report on International Understanding. Washington, D.C.: Committee on International Relations, American Association of Colleges for Teacher Education, 1963. Pp. 91.

   The papers included were presented at the Stanford University conference, March 28-30, 1963. They assess the educational investment needs of the Pacific area. Discussion group reports on various aspects of the central theme are also included. In general, the contents reflect a growing awareness of the social, economic, and political problems that beset educational development.

766. Enarson, Harold L. "The Successes and Failures of AID." (See No. 667.)

767. _____. "The Universities' Stake in the Developing Nations," Educational Record, XLV (Winter, 1964), 27-32. Reprints available from Education and World Affairs.

The United States has participated in international education primarily by admitting foreign students to our institutions. However, opening doors to students from developing areas is not enough. "In the last analysis, every nation must provide for the education of its own youth." Thus, it is imperative to help build strong educational systems abroad: this can be done in two ways: (a) by helping countries shape appropriate strategies for educational investment, and (b) by helping modernize existing universities in the developing nations.

768. Engineering for the Developing Countries. Washington, D.C.: National Academy of Sciences and National Research Council, 1961.

769. Evans, Luther H. "United States' Educational Activities Overseas," Overseas, III (November, 1963), 10-13.

770. Expanded Programme of Technical Assistance. (64.II.H.2.) New York: Technical Assistance Board, United Nations Secretariat, 1964. Pp. 20.

771. Fei, Edward. "Programs for Pakistan, Overseas, I (December, 1961), 20-25.

772. A Foreign Student Program for the Developing Countries During the Coming Decade. (See No. 394.)

773. Fraser, Stewart E. "Residential Academic Centers for International Education: A

Proposal for Their Establishment in the United States," <u>Peabody Journal of Education</u>, XLIII (March, 1966), 265-70.

774. Gelband, Carla S. "University Contract Programs: Education Support to Developing Nations." Mimeo., American Council on Education, 1961. Pp. 33. (Out of print.)

775. Glick, Philip Milton. <u>The Administration of Technical Assistance; Growth in the Americas</u>. Chicago: University of Chicago Press, 1957. Pp. 390.

In this study of the administrative organization and procedures of the United States, the United Nations, and the Organization of American States in Latin America, the author warns the universities that different types of contracts will necessitate different types of program responsibilities and relationships. ICA probably attempted too much supervision of university-to-university contracts but too little of other kinds of contracts.

776. Hamblin, F. N. "Western Nigeria Modernizes Teacher Education: The Ohio University Contract," <u>Changes in Teacher Education: An Appraisal</u>. Official Report, 18th National Commission on Teacher Education and Professional Standards Conference, June 25-28, 1963. Washington, D.C.: National Education Association, 1964, pp. 479-88.

*777. Harbison, Frederick H. "Education for Development," <u>Scientific American</u>, CCIX (September, 1963), 140-47. Reprints available from Education and World Affairs.

After reviewing educational development in Nyasaland, Colombia, China, and Egypt, five generalizations are set forth: (a) A strong correlation exists between educational development and economic productivity. (b) Education is not a sufficient guarantee of national prosperity. (c) Each country must pursue a balanced program related to its needs. (d) Educational goals and investments must be realistically shaped to the level of economic development. (e) Education creates an increasing demand for education.

*778. _____, and Myers, Charles A. <u>Education Manpower, and Economic Growth: Strategies of Human Resource Development</u>. New York: McGraw-Hill Book Co., Inc., 1964. Pp. 229.

This landmark volume is explicitly policy-oriented--"a blueprint for action." Using quantitative data, the authors have grouped countries into four categories: underdeveloped, partially developed, semiadvanced, and advanced. The problems of education are then discussed in relation to the prevalent economic, social, and political problems of each category. Special attention is given to the relationship between human-resource development and economic growth.

*779. _____, and _____ (eds.). <u>Manpower and Education; Country Studies in Economic Development</u>. New York: McGraw-Hill Book Co., Inc., 1965. Pp. 343.

The essays included discuss "the processes of human resource development and their relationship to economic growth." A more detailed account of certain countries is possible than the above volume, <u>Education, Manpower, and Economic Growth</u>, allowed.

780. Hart, Henry C. <u>Campus India; An Appraisal of American College Programs in India</u>. East Lansing: Michigan State University Press, 1961. Pp. 217.

After relating a history of United States college work in India and the general contemporary cultural content, the author candidly describes recent projects of eight United States colleges and universities. Several important insights on government, foundation, and administrative problems are recorded.

781. Heller, Walter W. "Men, Money, and Materials," <u>Educational Record</u>, XLIV (January, 1963), 12-16.

Recent studies on the role of the human resource in economic development have impressively demonstrated its crucial importance. The author suggests several policy shifts in development schemes: (a) more emphasis upon human capital development, (b) more middle level education, (c) creation of wage structures based on market forces to provide incentives, (d) more training, as opposed to general education.

782. Humphrey, Richard A. "International Education and the National Interest," <u>Graduate Comment</u>, (Wayne State University), VIII (Fall, 1964), 12-16.

783. _____. <u>The Role of American Higher Education in Relation to Developing Areas</u>. Report of the Conference on University Contracts Abroad. Washington, D.C.: American Council on Education, 1961.

This publication contains the principal addresses of the 6th Annual Conference, held in Washington, D.C., November 9, 1960. The contributions are directed toward human resource development and institution building, the contract device as a business arrangement, and the future for university programs abroad. A concluding offering by W. W. Rostow is titled, "The American Agenda in the Underdeveloped Areas."

*784. <u>International Rural Development</u>. Washington, D.C.: Agency for International Development, United States Department of State, 1964. Pp. 185.

Proceedings of the Conference on International Rural Development held in Washington, D.C., July 27-28, 1964, co-sponsored by the Agency for International Development, the United States Department of Agriculture, and the Association of State Universities and Land-Grant Colleges. The lengthy report contains committee recommendations and conference discussions on the following topics: country planning and execution, project planning and execution, development of personnel and institutions, and contractual arrangements.

785. Jacobson, Willard J. "Science Education and Technical Cooperation with Special Reference to Afghanistan," <u>Science Education</u>, XLIII (April, 1959), 245-56.

786. James, H. Thomas. "Problems in Administration and Finance When National Goals Become Primary." (See No. 667.)

787. Lacy, Dan M. "Cultural Exchanges Involving Institutions of Higher Learning," Educational Record, XXXVII (April, 1956), 118-22.

   The author speaks of developing education by the flow of books and the strengthening of libraries.

788. Leavitt, Howard B. "U.S. Technical Assistance to Latin American Education," Phi Delta Kappan, XLV (January, 1964), 220-25.

*789. Marvel, William W. "The Place of Education and Human Resource Development in Foreign Assistance." Report on a conference sponsored by the Carnegie Corporation, at Williamsburg, Virginia, April 8-10, 1962. New York: Carnegie Corp., 1962. Available from Education and World Affairs.

   The essential elements of a strategy for educational assistance are discussed. (a) Education serves a variety of ends and goals. (b) Any condition placed by the donor on the giving of financial aid should have the sole purpose of contributing to educational advance. (c) No matter what the segment or level of the educational system being aided, external assistance will be only a fraction of total educational expenditure in that country. (d) Any action taken precludes other possibilities for action. (e) National educational planning should grow out of manpower requirements. (f) Educational planning must be integrated with other aspects of national development planning. (g) Priorities should be arranged between the domestic and import sides of educational growth. (h) Priorities are also needed between formal education and non-school training. (i) The various levels and parts of the educational system must be integrated. (j) There are important decisions with regard to expanding the existing system and allowing experimentation. (k) The problem of educational content must not be neglected. (l) The West must mobilize its organizations, knowledge, and personnel.

790. Mooney, Francis E., Jr. "United States-Indonesian Cooperation in Higher Education: 1950-1961," *Journal of Higher Education*, XXXIV (February, 1963), 94-96.

The programs discussed were conducted under contracts between United States and Indonesian universities; all involved exchange of personnel between the institutions. Programs included the fields of agriculture, medicine, business, technical training, and college administration for the purposes of helping to train Indonesians to run their own institutions, helping to revise college curricula, providing supplies, and creating a respect for American higher education.

791. Mosher, Arthur Theodore. *Technical Cooperation in Latin American Agriculture*. Chicago: University of Chicago Press, 1957. Pp. 449.

792. Mosher, Frederick C. *The Administrative Science Program at Bologna*. Berkeley: Bureau of Public Administration, University of California, 1959. Pp. 36.

793. Myers, Charles Nash. *Education and National Development in Mexico*. ("Research Report Series," No. 106.) Princeton, N.J.: Industrial Relations Section, Department of Economics, Princeton University, 1965. Pp. 147.

794. "A New Basis for Technical Assistance Through Colleges and Universities." (See No. 689.)

795. *Opportunities for Cooperative Educational Programs in Africa*. A Report of five representatives of the Associated Colleges of the Midwest who visited four countries in Africa in the summer of 1962. Chicago: Associated Colleges of the Midwest, 1963.

796. Pett, Dennis W. "Communications Media Report from Nigeria," USAID/Indiana University Communications Media Project. *Audio Visual Instruction*, IX (November, 1964), 618-19.

797. Porter, Willis P. "Education for Economic Development in India and Pakistan." (See No. 667.)

798. _____. "Educational Needs of Southeast Asia," American Association of Colleges for Teacher Education Yearbook: 1961. 14th Yearbook, Annual Meeting, Chicago, 1961, pp. 83-98.

799. Prewitt, Charles W. "Science Education in Burma and the Fulbright Program," Science Education, XLIII (April, 1959), 257-63.

800. Reining, Henry, Jr. The Fourth Dimension: The Administration of Development and the University's Role. ("Comparative Public Administration Special Series," No. 3.) Chicago: Comparative Administration Group, American Society for Public Administration, 1964. Pp. 14.

*801. Robinson, Mary E. Education for Social Change: Establishing Institutes of Public and Business Administration Abroad. Washington, D.C.: Brookings Institution, 1961. Pp. 90.

At the request of the Public Administration Division of the International Cooperation Administration, Brookings Institution conducted a conference which provided the basis of this report "on the process of establishing and developing public and business administration institutes in countries abroad and the significance of this program as education for social change." The report borrows from an extensive technical assistance literature related to the preparation of public and business administrators and integrates this literature with data from numerous university contract experiences. Numerous recommendations and an excellent bibliography are included.

802. The Role of Universities in Technical Cooperation. Washington, D.C.: Special Policy Committee on Technical Cooperation, National Planning Association, 1955. Pp. 23.

The merits and disadvantages of university-to-university and university-to-government contracts are noted. Latin American programs are grouped and discussed under the following headings: operations in host countries, training nationals of host countries, and training of United States nationals for technical cooperation.

803. Rose, Alvin W. "Institution-Building in the New Nations: An Experience in the Congo (Toward a Frame of Reference for Educational Intervention in Transitional Societies)." Presented at the Conference on Education and the Modernizing of Nations, Detroit, September 24-25, 1964. Co-sponsored by the Commission on International Education of the American Council on Education and Wayne State University. Mimeo. Pp. 25.

The author presents six broad social characteristics requisite for notable advances in modernization: (a) symbols of national identification, (b) institutional structures for nation-wide information accumulation, (c) channels for role and cultural redefinition, (d) local institutions for social participation and decision-making, (e) facilities for channeling the flow of ideas and resources from elsewhere into the society, (f) an elite with values assuring the use of these means to reach modernizing goals. A discussion follows each point on the ways and means universities might participate in the creation of these prerequisites for development.

804. Roucek, Joseph S. "Is South America Making Progress?" (See No. 667.)

805. Ruffner, Ralph W. "American Educational Aid for National Development," Teachers College Record, LXII (February, 1961), 348-55.

A former ICA official discusses the role of the United States in advising nations, teaching foreign nationals, and giving material assistance.

806. _____. "Technical Cooperation in Education Through the International Cooperation Administration," Higher Education, XVI (April, 1960), 7-12.

807. Samper, Armando. Technical Cooperation in Latin America: A Case Study of Cooperation in Secondary Education in Chile. With a statement by the National Planning Association

Special Policy Committee on Technical Cooperation. Washington, D.C.: The Association, 1957. Pp. 82.

808. Scigliano, Robert G., and Fox, Guy H. Technical Assistance in Vietnam: The Michigan State University Experience. ("Praeger Special Studies in International Economics and Development.") New York: Frederick A. Praeger, Publishers, 1965. Pp. 78.

An historical account of one of the largest technical assistance programs conducted by an American university, the purpose of which was to assist police and security services of Vietnam. The authors emphasize the impact of the program upon cooperating Vietnamese agencies and the relations of Michigan State University with other American agencies and with the Vietnamese. The weaknesses of the project are also discussed.

809. Smith, Bruce L. Indonesian-American Cooperation in Higher Education. East Lansing: Institute of Research on Overseas Programs, Michigan State University, 1960. Pp. 133.

An extensive history of Indonesian higher education is followed by an analysis of the current situation. Next, Indonesian-American university relations are discussed under such headings as (a) general structure of the affiliations including the roles of top policymakers, administrators, and professors involved; (b) campus and overseas coordination; (c) special problems of planning and scheduling; and (d) recommendations.

810. Smuckler, Ralph H. "Michigan State University Vietnam Project," Institute of International Education: News Bulletin, XXXV (May, 1960), 2-6.

*811. _____. "University Responsibilities and International Development Research." Presented at the American Council on Education Seminar on "University Goals and Responsibilities in Foreign Operations," May 12-13, 1965.

An outstanding essay on the need for expanded

research related to development. Several suggestions and recommendations, plus reviews of relevant literature, are presented in four categories of research needs:

> (1) Studies of technical assistance administration and programming--including research on administration and operation of technical assistance and aid projects; overseas personnel matters; evaluation, etc. (2) Research to facilitate development programming and planning--including manpower studies, industry feasibility studies, surveys of school systems, soil and natural resource surveys, various types of data compilations, etc. (3) Research on development and change processes--including social scientific studies of institution building, behavioral studies, economic analyses, etc. (4) Research leading to scientific or technical innovation--including studies involving agricultural sciences, public health and medical personnel, engineers and scientists, etc.

812. Spence, Ralph B. "Teacher Education in Afghanistan," Educational Forum, XXVI (January, 1962), 143-53.

813. Storm, William B., and Gable, Richard W. "Technical Assistance in Higher Education: An Iranian Illustration," Educational Record, XLI (April, 1960), 175-82.

814. Taper, B. "National Development Through International Education," 5th Conference on International Education, Institute of International Education, Overseas, III (May, 1964), 2-20.

815. Thomas, R. Murray. "Guided Study in Indonesian Universities," Journal of Higher Education, XXXIV (May, 1963), 256-62.

The discussion is based principally upon the Indonesian work of the University of California Medical School.

816. Vent, Myron H. "AID and AUB: Partners in Middle East Development," Higher Education, XIX (April, 1963), 8-12.

817. Witt, Lawrence. "Towards an International Dimension in Agricultural Economics," *Journal of Farm Economics*, XLI (May, 1959), 211-20.

PART VII

RESOURCE MATERIALS

CHAPTER **18** HANDBOOKS, GUIDES, AND REFERENCE WORKS

818. <u>AID-Financed University Contracts</u>. (See No. 715.)

819. <u>American Agencies Interested in International Affairs</u>. New York: Council on Foreign Relations, 1964.

820. Barker, H. Kenneth (ed.). <u>AACTE Handbook of International Education Programs</u>. Washington, D.C.: American Association of Colleges for Teacher Education, 1963. Pp. 72.

 A guide for administrators in the field of international education. Designed with emphasis upon programs for teachers.

821. Buchler, M. Josephine, and Wang, Joan Parsons, (eds.). "Indiana University Directory of Faculty with International Interests." Mimeo., International Development Research Center, Indiana University, 1965. Pp. 93. (Out of print.)

 Brief biographies of faculty members with overseas experience. Four indexes were used: foreign research areas, subject index, faculty index, and language fluency index.

822. Cormack, Margaret L., <u>et al</u>. <u>The International Programs of American Universities</u>. Research sponsored by Education and World Affairs, and carried out at the Institute of Advanced Projects, East-West Center. East Lansing: Office of International Programs, Michigan State University, in press.

 An inventory of self-descriptions of American college and university international programs followed by an analysis of certain program characteristics.

823. Crabbs, Richard F. (ed.). "Survey of World Affairs Activities of Indiana University, 1963-64." Mimeo., University Committee on International Affairs, Indiana University, 1964. Pp. 51. (Out of print.)

824. Directory of Faculty Personnel with International Academic Interests 1963-64. Madison: University of Wisconsin, 1964. Pp. 115.

825. Directory of Professional Interests in Foreign Areas 1963-64. 2nd ed. Los Angeles: Institute of International and Foreign Studies, University of California, 1964. Pp. 126.

826. Educational and Cultural Diplomacy. (See No. 668.)

827. Educational and Cultural Exchange Opportunities. ("Department of State Publication," No. 7543, "International Information and Cultural Series," No. 83.) Washington, D.C.: United States Department of State, 1963. Pp. 27.

828. Flack, Michael J. Sources of Information on International Educational Activities; An Exploratory Survey. Prepared for the Commission on Education and International Affairs of the American Council on Education. Washington, D.C.: The Council, 1958. Pp. 114.

829. Foreign Policy Association and World Affairs Center. Careers in World Affairs: At Home and Abroad. Garden City, N.Y.: Doubleday & Co., Inc., 1961. Pp. 140.

830. Foreign Students in Catholic Colleges and Universities, 1962-1963. Washington, D.C.: National Catholic Educational Association, 1963.

831. Garraty, John A., and Adams, Walter. A Guide to Study Abroad: University Summer School, Tour, and Work-and-Study Programs. Introduction

HANDBOOKS, GUIDES, AND REFERENCE WORKS   173

by President Lyndon B. Johnson, Manhasset, N.Y.: Channel Press, 1963. Pp. 288.

832. Guide to Institutional Self-Study and the Evaluation of Overseas Educational Programs. Prepared by the Committee on Academic Programs Abroad and the Evaluation Project Committee of the Council on Student Travel. New York: Council on Student Travel, 1965. Pp. 48.

A bibliography is included.

*833. Handbook on International Study: For Foreign Nationals. 4th ed. New York: Institute of International Education, 1965.

A discussion of education in the United States is followed by lists of accredited institutions, summer opportunities, awards and special programs, and organizations in the United States providing services to foreign nationals. A statistical appendix on educational exchange and an extensive bibliography are included.

*834. Handbook on International Study: For U.S. Nationals. 4th ed. New York: Institute of International Education, 1965.

A discussion of education abroad is followed by lists of awards and special programs, summer opportunities, and organizations in the United States providing services to United States nationals going abroad. A statistical appendix on educational exchange and an extensive bibliography are included.

835. IIE Services to Colleges and Universities. New York: Institute of International Education, 1963. Pp. 19.

*836. Intercultural Education; An Information Service of Education and World Affairs: Fellowships for Faculty and Students, Conferences, Bibliography. New York: Education and World Affairs, 1965. Pp. 75.

837. International Educational, Cultural, and Related Activities for African Countries

South of the Sahara. Washington, D.C.: Bureau of Educational and Cultural Affairs, United States Department of State, 1961. Pp. 321.

A collection of facts concerning numerous programs of United States government and international agencies and private organizations.

*838. Moses, Larry (comp.). Language and Area Study Programs in American Universities. Washington, D.C.: External Research Staff, Bureau of Intelligence and Research, United States Department of State, 1964. Pp. 162.

Listed and described are 153 programs leading to graduate degrees and a sampling of undergraduate programs of four-year schools. Faculty listings and a language index are included.

839. The NAFSA Directory. New York: National Association for Foreign Student Affairs, annually.

Membership Directory of the National Association for Foreign Student Affairs, Fulbright Program Advisers, Teachers of English as a Foreign Language, Foreign Student Admission Officers, and Community Hospitality Program Leaders of U.S. Institutions of Higher Education.

840. 1965-66 Teacher Exchange Opportunities. Washington, D.C.: Office of Education, United States Department of Health, Education, and Welfare, 1964. Pp. 34.

Lists summer seminars, teaching, research, and study opportunities for American elementary, secondary, and college teachers under the International Educational Exchange Program of the United States Department of State and the Office of Education, United States Department of Health, Education, and Welfare.

*841. Open Doors. New York: Institute of International Education, annually.

This report offers the most comprehensive statistical information readily available on the

HANDBOOKS, GUIDES, AND REFERENCE WORKS 175

subject of international educational exchange between the United States and foreign countries and institutions.

842. Palmer, Archie M., and Kruzas, Anthony T. (eds.). Research Centers Directory. (See No. 124.)

843. Rhoades, Margaret M. (comp.). Research Centers on the Developing Areas. Prepared for the Agency for International Development. Washington, D.C.: External Research Staff, Bureau of Intelligence and Research, United States Department of State, 1964. Pp. 131.

    Identifies and describes 140 research centers and current research projects.

844. Semester and Academic Year Programs. ("Students Abroad Series.") New York: Council on Student Travel, Inc., annually.

845. Some U.S. Government Agencies Engaged in International Activities. Washington, D.C.: Bureau of Educational and Cultural Affairs, United States Department of State, 1963. Pp. 98.

*846. Study Abroad: International Directory of Fellowships, Scholarships, and Awards Compiled by UNESCO; 1964-1966. New York: United Nations Educational, Scientific and Cultural Organization, Publications Center, 1963. Pp. 648.

847. Summer Study Abroad. New York: Institute of International Education, annually.

848. Summer Study, Travel, and Work Programs, 1966. ("Students Abroad Series.") New York: Council on Student Travel, Inc., annually.

849. Teaching Abroad. Paris: United Nations Educational, Scientific and Cultural Organization, annually.

    A world-wide listing of teachers and scholars willing to teach abroad.

*850. UNESCO Handbook of International Exchanges.

Paris: United Nations Educational, Scientific and Cultural Organization, 1965. Pp. 861.

Information concerning agencies and programs in international educational exchange.

851. U.S. Interagency Directory: Key Contacts for Planning and Development of Educational, Cultural, Scientific, and Technical Exchange Programs. Washington, D.C.: Policy Review and Coordination Staff, Bureau of Educational and Cultural Affairs, United States Department of State, 1965.

*852. U.S. Non-Profit Organizations, Voluntary Agencies, Missions, and Foundations Participating in Technical Assistance Abroad: A Directory, 1964. New York: Technical Assistance Clearing House of the American Council of Voluntary Agencies for Foreign Service, Inc., 1964. Pp. 759.

853. Vacations Abroad. New York: United Nations Educational, Scientific and Cultural Organization, Publications Center, annually.

Information on summer courses, study tours, youth centers, work camps, and student facilities in all parts of the world.

854. White, Aurilla. Annexes to Guidelines for Evaluating the Participant Training Program. Prepared for the International Cooperation Administration. Washington, D.C.: Bureau of Social Science Research, Inc., 1960. Pp. 38.

855. _____. Survey Guidelines for Evaluation of Participant Training Programs. Prepared for the International Cooperation Administration. Washington, D.C.: Bureau of Social Science Research, Inc., 1960. Pp. 32.

856. Winning the Cold War: The U.S. Ideological Offensive. Hearings before the Subcommittee on International Organizations and Movements, Committee on Foreign Affairs, United States House of Representatives, May 25, 1965. House Report 368. (89th Cong., 1st sess.; "Overseas

HANDBOOKS, GUIDES, AND REFERENCE WORKS   177

Programs of Private Nonprofit American Organizations," Report No. 3; Pursuant to H.R. 84.) Washington, D.C.: Government Printing Office, 1965. Pp. 565.

Listed are 582 organizations with overseas programs including several programs of colleges and universities.

857. <u>Work, Study, Travel Abroad: A Guide to Summer Travel Opportunities for American Students.</u> New York: Educational Travel, Inc., United States National Student Association, annually.

CHAPTER 19 BIBLIOGRAPHIES

858. <u>Bibliography: Publications in Comparative and International Education</u>. Washington, D.C.: Division of International Education, Office of Education, United States Department of Health, Education, and Welfare.

    Editions from the years 1956-60. Short annotations.

859. Brickman, William W. <u>Foreign Students in the United States: A Selected and Annotated Bibliography</u>. Princeton, N.J.: College Entrance Examination Board, 1963.

    A brief pamphlet of short, critical annotations on historical works, research studies on admission, placement and guidance of foreign students, admission and placement, guidance and counseling, general surveys and miscellaneous works, comparative writings, bibliographies, reference works, and periodicals.

860. _____. "Selected Bibliography of the History of International Relations in Higher Education." Mimeo., University of Pennsylvania, 1964. Pp. 13.

861. Cieslak, Edward C. "A Bibliography; Selected and Annotated," <u>Phi Delta Kappan</u>, XXXV (May, 1954), 349-56.

    Works on educational exchange and comparative education are included.

862. Cormack, Margaret L. <u>An Evaluation of Research on Educational Exchange</u>. (See No. 300.)

BIBLIOGRAPHIES   179

863.   Cotner, Thomas E. International Educational
       Exchange: A Selected Bibliography. (OE-14066.)
       Washington, D.C.: Office of Education, United
       States Department of Health, Education, and
       Welfare, 1961. Pp. 117.

       Somewhat updates and greatly expands the 1951
       and 1954 editions.

864.   _____, Grissom, John W., and Knapp, Frank A.
       A Partial Bibliography of Materials Related
       to International Education. Washington, D.C.:
       Office of Education, United States Department
       of Health, Education, and Welfare, 1954.
       Pp. 104.

865.   Cross-Cultural Education: A Bibliography of
       Government-Sponsored and Private Research on
       Foreign Students and Trainees in the U.S. and
       in Other Countries--1946-1964. Washington,
       D.C.: External Research Staff, Bureau of
       Intelligence and Research, United States
       Department of State, April, 1965. Pp. 61.

       Items are arranged by origin of sponsorship:
       United Nations Educational, Scientific and
       Cultural Organization, various agencies of the
       United States government, and private research.
       The latter division is subdivided by forms of
       publication.

866.   Handbook on International Study: For Foreign
       Nationals. (See No. 833.)

867.   Handbook on International Study: For U.S.
       Nationals. (See No. 834.)

868.   Hill-Murray, Mildred, Carey, Marjorie L., and
       Tandler, Fredrika M. Selected Bibliography
       of Recent Materials Related to International
       Education. ("Information on Education Around
       the World Series," No. OE-14034-40.) Washing-
       ton, D.C.: Office of Education, United States
       Department of Health, Education, and Welfare,
       1960. Pp. 17.

869.   International Education. Claremont, Calif.:
       College Student Personnel Institute, 1962.

Annotated here is a collection of recent books, pamphlets, and articles organized under the following headings: international education; implications for curricula; Americans studying abroad; foreign students in the United States; and bibliographies, fact books, handbooks, and other reference sources.

870. <u>International Educational and Cultural Exchange; A Selective Bibliography of Materials on Both Governmental and Private Programs.</u> Washington, D.C.: Policy Review and Research Staff, Bureau of Educational and Cultural Affairs, United States Department of State, 1963. Pp. 15.

871. <u>Inventory of Recent Publications and Research Studies in the Field of International Educational and Cultural Affairs.</u> Washington, D.C.: CU Reference Center, Policy Review and Coordination Staff, Bureau of Educational and Cultural Affairs, United States Department of State.
    1st issue, June, 1964. Pp. 14.
    2nd issue, October, 1964. Pp. 16.
    3rd issue, April, 1965. Pp. 12.

872. Jacobsen, Joseph M. <u>A Study of Three Related Research Projects.</u> (See No. 304.)

873. Klineberg, Otto. "Research on International Exchanges in Education, Science and Culture." (See No. 306.)

874. Legters, Lyman H. (comp.). <u>Bibliography of Language and Area Studies.</u> Foreign Area Materials Center Occasional Publication Series. New York: The University of the State of New York, in press.

875. Mestenhauser, Josef A. (ed.). <u>Research in Programs for Foreign Students: A Report of the Waldenwoods Seminar.</u> (See No. 307.)

876. Porter, Robert D. (ed.). <u>Selected Studies in Intercultural Education.</u> (See No. 308.)

877. Putnam, Ivan, Jr. <u>The Foreign Student</u>

BIBLIOGRAPHIES   181

       Adviser's Bookshelf. New York: National
       Association for Foreign Student Affairs, 1960.

878.   *Research in International Education*. (See
       No. 309.)

879.   Robinson, Mary E. *Education for Social
       Change: Establishing Institutes of Public
       and Business Administration Abroad*. (See
       No. 801.)

880.   Schmidt, Liselotte. "Study Abroad: A Bib-
       liography," *Comparative Education Review*, V
       (October, 1961), 142-55.

       An excellent collection of short annotations.

881.   Warmbrunn, Werner (ed.). *Research Studies in
       Intercultural Education: Reviews and Implica-
       tions for Exchange of Persons*. (See No. 313.)

882.   Weidner, Edward. *The World Role of Universi-
       ties*. (See No. 39.)

APPENDIX

APPENDIX A ORGANIZATIONS WITH
MAJOR INTERESTS IN HIGHER
EDUCATION AND WORLD AFFAIRS

This directory does not include the associations of individual nations, the international committees and scholarship programs of individual colleges and universities, nor many of the general professional organizations and foundations. These groups are well described in the directories listed in the Resource Materials section (p. 169) of the Bibliography.

> Advancement and Placement Institute
> Box 99, Greenpoint Station
> Brooklyn 22, New York
>
> African-American Institute
> 345 East 46th Street
> New York, New York 10017
>
> 1346 Connecticut Avenue N.W.
> Washington, D.C. 20006
>
> African-American Students Foundation
> 375 Park Avenue
> New York 22, New York
>
> African Scholarship Program of American Universities (ASPAU)
> 75 Mount Auburn Street
> Cambridge 38, Massachusetts
>
> African Studies Association
> 409 West 117th Street
> New York, New York 10027
>
> American Association of Colleges for Teacher Education. Committee on International Relations
> 1201 16th Street N.W.
> Washington, D.C. 20036

American Association for Health, Physical
Education, and Recreation. International
Relations Section
  1201 16th Street N.W.
  Washington, D.C. 20036

American Association for the Advancement
of Slavic Studies
  1207 West Oregon Street
  University of Illinois
  Urbana, Illinois 61801

American Council on Education
  1785 Massachusetts Avenue N.W.
  Washington, D.C. 20036

American Council of Voluntary Agencies
for Foreign Service, Inc. Technical
Assistance Clearing House
  44 East 23rd Street
  New York 18, New York

American Field Service
  313 East 43rd Street
  New York, New York 10017

American Friends of the Middle East
  1607 New Hampshire Avenue N.W.
  Washington, D.C. 20009

Regional Offices:

  225 East 46th Street
  New York, New York 10017

  116 South Michigan
  Chicago, Illinois 60603

  323 Geary Street
  San Francisco, California 94102

American Friends Service Committee
  160 North 15th Street
  Philadelphia, Pennsylvania 19102

American Overseas Educators Organization,
Inc.
  725 South Division Street
  Ann Arbor, Michigan

APPENDIX A

American-Scandinavian Foundation
127 East 73rd Street
New York, New York 10021

American Universities Field Staff
366 Madison Avenue
New York, New York

Asia Foundation
P. O. Box 3223
San Francisco, California 94119

Association for Asian Studies
48 Lane Hall
University of Michigan
Ann Arbor, Michigan 48104

Association of American Law Schools
Committee on Foreign Exchanges
1755 Massachusetts Avenue N.W.
Washington, D.C. 20036

Carnegie Endowment for International Peace
Committee on Foreign Affairs Personnel
345 East 46th Street
Washington, D.C. 10017

Committee on Educational Interchange Policy
(See Institute of International Education)

Comparative Education Society
c/o Franklin Parker, Secretary
Box 338
University of Oklahoma
Norman, Oklahoma

Conference Board of Associated Research
Councils. Committee on International
Exchange of Persons
2101 Constitution Avenue
Washington, D.C. 20418

Coordinating Secretariat of National
Unions of Students (COSEC)
Post Box 36
Leiden, The Netherlands

Council for Educational Cooperation
with Africa
1 East 67th Street
New York, New York

Council on Student Travel
  777 United Nations Plaza
  New York, New York 10017

East-West Center for Cultural and Technical Interchange Between East and West
  University of Hawaii
  Honolulu, Hawaii 96822

Education and World Affairs
  522 Fifth Avenue
  New York, New York 10036

Educational Council for Foreign Medical Graduates
  1633 Central Street
  Evanston, Illinois 60201

Experiment in International Living, Inc.
  Putney, Vermont 05346

Regional Offices:

  Suite 1801, Henry Hudson Hotel
  New York, New York 10019

  811 Dupont Circle Building
  1346 Connecticut Avenue N.W.
  Washington, D.C. 20036

  291 Geary Street
  San Francisco, California 94102

  33 Garden Street
  Cambridge, Massachusetts 02138

Ford Foundation
  477 Madison Avenue
  New York, New York 10022

Foreign Area Fellowship Program
  444 Madison Avenue
  New York, New York 10022

Foreign Policy Association
  345 East 46th Street
  New York, New York 10017

Hazen Foundation. Committee on the College and World Affairs
  400 Prospect Street
  New Haven, Connecticut

APPENDIX A

Institute of International Education
809 United Nations Plaza
New York, New York 10017

IIE Regional Offices:

116 South Michigan Avenue
Chicago, Illinois 60603

1600 Sherman Street
Denver, Colorado 80203

1520 Texas Avenue
Houston, Texas 77002

291 Geary Street
San Francisco, California 94102

1530 P Street N.W.
Washington, D.C. 20005

IIE Overseas Offices:

Cargen House
Harambee Avenue (P.O. Box 5869)
Nairobi, Kenya

Maximo Abril 599
Apartado 300
Lima, Peru

78 North Sathorn Road
Bangkok, Thailand

Reid Hall
4 Rue de Chevreuse
Paris, France

International Association for Educational
and Vocational Information (IAEVI)
29 Rue d'Ulm
Paris, 5, France

International Association of Universities
6 Rue Franklin
Paris, France

International Bureau of Education
Palais Wilson
Geneva, Switzerland

International Federation of Organizations for Scholastic Correspondences and Exchanges (FIOCES)
 29 Rue d'Ulm
 Paris, France

International Institute for Educational Planning
 7 Rue Eugene-Delacroix
 Paris 16e, France

International Social Science Council Committee on Cross-Cultural Education
 6 Rue Franklin (UNESCO Annexe)
 Paris 16e, France

Middle East Institute
 1761 North Street, N.W.
 Washington, D.C. 20036

Modern Language Association
 4 Washington Place
 New York, New York 10003

National Academy of Sciences, National Research Council. Office of International Relations
 2101 Constitution Avenue N.W.
 Washington, D.C. 20418

National Association for Foreign Student Affairs (formerly National Association of Foreign Student Advisers)
 809 United Nations Plaza
 New York, New York 10017

National Association of State Universities and Land-Grant Colleges
 1785 Massachusetts Avenue N.W.
 Washington, D.C. 20036

National Catholic Educational Association International Student Program
 1785 Massachusetts Avenue N.W.
 Washington, D.C. 20036

National Education Association. Division of Educational Travel
 1201 16th Street N.W.
 Washington, D.C. 20036

APPENDIX A 191

National Science Foundation. Office of
International Science Activities
  1800 G Street N.W.
  Washington, D.C. 20550

Organization of American States. Exchange of Persons Service
  General Secretariat
  Pan American Union
  Washington, D.C. 20006

Overseas Education Fund of the League of Women Voters
  1026 17th Street N.W.
  Washington, D.C. 20036

Overseas Educational Service
  522 Fifth Avenue
  New York, New York 10036

Phelps-Stokes Fund
  297 Park Avenue South
  New York 10, New York

Society for International Development
  1346 Connecticut Avenue N.W.
  Washington, D.C. 20036

United Nations Educational, Scientific and Cultural Organization (UNESCO)
  Place de Fontenoy
  Paris 7, France

  2201 United Nations Building
  New York, New York

UNESCO Liaison Office
  1028 Connecticut Avenue N.W.
  Washington, D.C. 20036

United Nations Special Fund. Bureau of Operations. Training Division
  New York, New York 10017

UNITED STATES GOVERNMENT ORGANIZATIONS
Washington, D.C.

Atomic Energy Commission. Division of International Affairs. Training and Education Branch
  1717 H Street N.W.   20545

Department of Agriculture. Foreign Agricultural Service for Training Division
  14th & Independence Avenue S.W.   20250

Department of Defense
  The Pentagon   20301

Department of State
  2201 C Street N.W.   20520

The following have the State Department address:

  Agency for International Development. International Training Division

  Board of Foreign Scholarships. Operations Staff

  Bureau of Educational and Cultural Affairs

  Bureau of Intelligence and Research. External Research Staff (administers the Interdepartmental Foreign Area Research Coordination Group, FAR)

  Interagency Council of International Educational and Cultural Affairs

  U.S. Advisory Commission on International and Cultural Affairs

  U.S. National Commission for UNESCO

Office of Education. Bureau of International Education
  400 Maryland Avenue N.W.   20202

APPENDIX A   193

   Peace Corps
      806 Connecticut Avenue N.W.   20525

   Public Health Service. Division of
   International Health. Education and
   Training Division
      330 Independence Avenue S.W.   20201

   U.S. Information Agency. Information
   Center Services
      1776 Pennsylvania Avenue N.W.   20547

   United States National Student Association
      2115 S Street N.W.   20008

   Regional Office:

      Educational Travel, Inc.
      265 Madison Avenue
      New York, New York   10016

   World Assembly of Youth
      66 Rue St. Bernard
      Brussels, Belgium

   U.S. Affiliate:

      U.S. Council of the National Social
      Welfare Assembly
      345 East 46th Street
      New York, New York   10017

   World Confederation of Organizations
   of the Teaching Profession
      1227 16th Street N.W.
      Washington, D.C.   20036

   World University Roundtable (WUR)
   International Section
      P. O. Box 4800-K
      Tucson, Arizona

   World University Service
      20 West 40th Street
      New York, New York   10018

AUTHOR INDEX

AUTHOR INDEX

(References are to entry numbers)

Abrams, Freda, 364
Abrams, Irwin, 314-17, 364
Adams, Donald K., 667, 675
Adams, John Clarke, 209-10
Adams, Richard N., 747
Adams, Walter, 326, 653, 748, 831
African Language and Area Center, 141
Albert, Ethel M., 114
Allen, Herman R., 1
American Assembly, 658
American Association of Colleges for Teacher Education, 55, 765
American Council on Education, 18, 32, 383, 719
American Embassy, Bonn, Germany, 577
American Embassy, New Delhi, India, 578
American Embassy, Vienna, Austria, 579
American Institute for Research, Inc., 580
Anderson, C. Arnold, 675, 667
Anderson, George L., 143, 162
Andrews, Wade H., 581
Andrus, J. Russell, 750
Angell, Melvin, 538
Arensberg, Conrad M., 200
Armajani, Yahya, 89
Armstrong, Robert G., 137
Arndt, C. O., 43

Arnold, Ruth, 562
Asher, Robert E., 735
Associated Colleges of the Midwest, 795
Association of American Colleges, 123
Asthana, Hari S., 582
Awasthi, S. P., 367
Axelrod, Joseph, 90

Bailey, Jackson H., 91
Bailyn, Lotte, 467, 483
Ballinger, Stanley E., 17
Bang, Katherine C., 272, 368
Barakat, Mohamed Khalifa, 583
Bardis, P. D., 459
Barker, H. Kenneth, 76, 667, 820
Barnett, Norman N., 259
Barnett, Vincent M., Jr., 201-2
Barton, R. D., 203
Battsek, M., 320
Baumgartner, Leona, 717
Beal, Harriet, 369
Beals, Ralph L., 313, 460, 487
Beasley, William G., 145
Beck, Robert H., 370
Beckmann, George M., 92, 95
Beebe, George A., 313, 371
Bell, David E., 718, 731
Benjamin, Harold R. W., 675
Bennett, John W., 114, 299, 461-64, 487, 584
Bennington College, 585
Berbusse, Edward J., 372

Berg, Sherwood O., 373
Berry, Paul L., 95
Bharagava, K. P., 586
Bidwell, Percy W., 44-45
Bier, Jesse, 260
Bigelow, Donald N., 90, 93-95
Bigelow, Karl W., 78, 204, 752
Bigman, Stanley K., 587
Bingham, Woodbridge, 146
Bjerstedt, Ake, 467
Bjork, Robert, 675
Black, Cyril E., 191
Blackton, Charles S., 96
Bland, Sister Joan, 46
Blum, Robert, 272, 658, 730
Board of Foreign Scholarships, 280, 672
Boardman, Eugene Powers, 147
Bolivian Institute of Public Opinion Research, 588
Bolling, Landrum R., 2
Bonilla, Frank, 589
Bordie, John G., 138
Borton, Hugh, 148
Bowles, Chester, 47
Bowles, Frank H., 3, 539
Bragdon, Helen, 32
Bray, Barbara, 481
Bremseth, Cameron F., 590-91
Bressler, Marvin, 313, 487-89
Brickman, William W., 285, 675, 859-60
Broadhurst, Martha Jean, 374
Bronfenbrenner, Martin, 753
Brown, Ina Corinne, 675
Brown, W. Norman, 95, 149-50
Brubacher, John S., 667
Bryant, William Cullen, II, 505
Buchler, M. Josephine, 821
Buehrig, Edward H., 48

Buist, Eleanor, 118
Buitron, Anibal, 205
Bumgartner, Louis E., 179
Bureau of Social Science Research, Inc., 354, 592-93, 595-97, 659
Burnor, Duane R., 470
Burns, Norman, 13
Bush, Gerald W., 240
Butts, R. Freeman, 17, 241, 754
Byrnes, Francis C., 206
Byrnes, Robert F., 97, 191-93, 261, 667

Cajoleas, Louis P., 49, 375
Caldwell, Lynton K., 207, 720
Caldwell, Oliver J., 50, 99, 272, 667, 675, 755
Carey, Marjorie L., 868
Carleton, William G., 51
Carnegie Endowment for International Peace, 228
Carnegie Foundation for the Advancement of Teaching, 4
Carson, George Barr, Jr., 191
Castagno, Alfonso A., 118
Cater, Douglass, 262
Catlin, Louella C., 540
Central Research Services, Inc., 599
Cerych, Ladislav, 756
Chambers, Clarke A., 272
Chen, Theodore H. E., 675
China Institute, 294
Christ, June R., 304, 379, 521
Chunn, Anthony F., 501
Cieslak, Edward C., 313, 376, 861
Clay, Lucius, 696
Clements, Forrest E., 600-1

AUTHOR INDEX

Cleveland, Harlan, 199, 208-10, 237
Cline, Howard F., 118, 180
Coan, Clark, 465, 602
Coelho, George V., 466-67
Cohen, Herman J., 660
Cohen, Maurice, 52
Cole, Fred, 53
Coleman, James S., 757
College Student Personnel Institute, 869
Colligan, Francis J., 286, 685
Committee on Educational Interchange Policy, see Institute of International Education
Committee on the University and World Affairs, 38
Committee to Strengthen the Security of the Free World, 696
Conference on Asian Affairs, 75
Conrad, Lawrence, 43
Converse, Elizabeth, 623
Cook, David R., 468
Cook, Donald B., 264
Cook, Stuart W., 304, 379, 467, 469, 521, 525
Coombs, Philip H., 380-81, 658, 662
Cooper, Robert L., 541
Cormack, Margaret L., 300, 382, 822
Cotner, Thomas E., 663-64, 759, 863-64
Council on Foreign Relations, 819
Council on Student Travel, 268, 832, 844, 848
Crabbs, Richard F., 823
Crane, Robert I., 151
Creel, Herrlee G., 152
Cullen, Arthur J., 184
Cullers, Robert M., 603-4
Cumberland, Charles C., 747

Cummings, Ivor G., 437
Curle, Adam, 760
Cussler, Margaret, 301

Dacso, Michael, 400
Danto, Arthur, 153
Darrah, L. B., 384
Davidsen, Oluf M., 487, 503, 522, 525
Davidson, Basil, 139
Davis, James M., 272, 385-87, 470, 496, 675, 694
Dawes, Norman, 265
Dean, James W., 471
Dean, Vera Micheles, 101
deBary, William Theodore, 95, 102, 154-58
Dembo, Miriam, 542
Deney, Nicole J., 264
Dersham, James F., 115
Deutsch, Steven E., 494
DeWitt, Nicholas, 667
Diab, Lutfy, 472
Diamond, Lorraine K., 543
Dizney, Henry F., 544
Dole, Arthur A., 501
Donahue, Francis M., 605
Donoghue, John, 281
Donovan, James A., Jr., 666
Dowling, Leo R., 523
Drucker, Peter F., 5
DuBois, Cora, 302, 313, 388, 474-75
Duge, Edna, 606
Dustan, Jane, 211

East-West Center, 822
Echols, John M., 159
Education and World Affairs, 6, 545, 554, 681, 712, 716, 836
Ehrman, Edith, 160
Ekman, Ernst, 56
Elder, Robert Ellsworth, 671
Elliott, Alan J. A., 264
Embree, Ainslie, 158

Enarson, Harold L., 667, 737, 766
Englund, David L., 242
Esman, Milton J., 212
Evans, Luther H., 769
Evans, P. C. C., 213
External Research Staff, see United States Bureau of Intelligence and Research
Ezell, Stiles D., 321

Fairbank, John K., 161
Fairchild, Mildred L., 214
Fairfield, Roy P., 243
Fayerweather, John, 215
Fei, Edward, 771
Feraru, Arthur, 391
Ferguson, Charles A., 95
Fife, Austin E., 104
Finch, Rogers B., 244
Fisher, Harold H., 194
Flack, Michael J., 828
Flapan, Maxwell, 105
Ford Foundation, 761
Foreign Policy Association, 829
Forman, Robert E., 627
Forstat, Reisha, 476
Forster, Kent, 57
Fox, Guy H., 808
Fox, Melvin J., 395
Frankel, Charles, 7, 674
Fraser, Stewart E., 675, 773
Freed, Marjorie, 322
Freeman, Stephen A., 95, 324-25
French, John R. P., Jr., 477
Frenz, Horst, 162
Fulbright, J. William, 272
Fuller, C. Dale, 216
Fuller, William A., Jr., 245

Gable, Richard W., 440, 813
Gange, John, 8
Gannon, Martin, 478

Gardner, John W., 721
Garraty, John A., 326, 748, 831
Garrison, Karl C., 58, 81
Gelband, Carla S., 774
German Institute for Public Opinion Research, 612
Gezi, Khalil Ismail, 479
Gibb, Sir Hamilton, 106
Gillett, Margaret, 396
Ginsberg, Mitchell I., 246
Glick, Philip Milton, 775
Golay, Frank H., 95
Goldman, Rene, 675
Goldsen, Rose K., 525
Goldstein, Marcia Gray, 398
Gollin, Albert E., 601
Goodwin, Leonard, 355
Gould, Samuel B., 327
Gouverneur, Isabel M., 546
Gray, Jack D., 217
Green, Walter, 480
Griffin, W. H., 356
Griffith, Ernest S., 218
Grissom, John W., 864
Group for the Advancement of Psychiatry, 239
Guggenheim, Michel, 328
Gullahorn, Jeanne E., 305, 329, 348, 357-61, 399, 494
Gullahorn, John T., 329, 348, 357-61, 399, 494

Hagberg, Gordon P., 272
Hagberg, Peter, 330
Halberstam, Jacob L., 400, 498
Hall, Edward T., 219-20
Haller, A. D., 481
Hallo, William W., 164
Halpern, Manfred, 187
Hamar, Clifford E., 107

AUTHOR INDEX

Hamblin, F. N., 776
Hamilton, D. Lee, 108
Haniotis, George V., 401
Hanson, Russell G., 470
Harari, Maurice, 402
Harbison, Frederick, 731, 777-78
Harrington, Fred Harvey, 9
Hart, Henry C., 780
Hartwell, Robert, 165
Harvard University, 761
Haskins, Lewis M., 331
Hauch, Charles C., 482
Havel, Joan, 304, 379
Haviland, H. Field, Jr., 677
Hayes, Samuel Perkins, 247
Hazen Foundation, 54
Heller, Walter W., 781
Henderson, Dan Fenno, 109
Henderson, Gregory, 403
Henry, David D., 10, 404
Henry, Edwin R., 229
Herman, Simon N., 303, 349-51
Higbee, Homer D., 405, 442
Hill-Murray, Mildred, 868
Hilsman, Roger, 730
Hodgson, Marshall, 188
Holden, John, 32
Holland, Kenneth, 264, 272, 738
Hooker, Gertrude S., 658
Hopson, Anna Lee, 525
Houle, Cyril O., 11
Houlihan, Marita, 442
Hountras, Peter Timothy, 547-49
Howell, Margaret A., 221
Hubbert, Erin, 680
Huerta, Czarina, 406
Hughes, Emmet John, 12
Hughes, Thomas L., 722
Humphrey, Norman D., 313, 460, 487
Humphrey, Richard A., 13, 222, 272, 723-24, 782-83

Hunnicutt, Clarence W., 14
Hurewitz, Jacob C., 189-90

Institute for Social Research, Oslo, 613
Institute of African-American Relations, 530
Institute of International Education, 263, 267, 274, 297, 309, 318, 343, 366, 389-90, 392-94, 397, 415, 425, 447, 457, 565, 697, 833-35, 841, 847
International Institute for Public Opinion and Market Research, 615
International Public Opinion Research, Inc., 616-18
International Research Associates, Inc., 619-20, 683
International Research Associates, Mexico, 621-22
Israel, Thomas S., 566
Iversen, Robert W., 248

Jackson, Frederick H., 95
Jacobsen, Joseph M., 304
Jacobson, Eugene H., 305, 494
Jacobson, Willard J., 785
James, H. Thomas, 667
Johnson, Harvey L., 182
Johnson, Walter, 685

Kaihara, Motosuke, 427
Katz, Joseph, 675
Kauffman, Joseph F., 249
Kaufmann, Fritz, 332
Kaulfers, Walter V., 550
Keeffe, Emily C., 623
Kehoe, Monika, 333
Kelman, Herbert C., 467, 483, 494

Kelsey, Clyde E., Jr., 19
Keppel, Francis, 667
Ketcham, Ralph L., 59
Kiell, Norman, 484
Kincaid, Harry V., 407
King, John A., Jr., 408
Kitchen, Robert W., Jr., 409
Kittler, Glenn D., 250
Klein, Roger H., 334
Klineberg, Otto, 306
Kling, Merle, 183
Klinger, M. R. B., 485, 675
Knapp, Frank A., 864
Koenig, Clara H., 551-52
Krueger, Anna Barbara, 486
Kruzas, Anthony T., 124
Kublin, Hyman, 118
Kumata, Hideya, 305
Kunhart, William E., 507
Kuppuswamy, B., 624

Lacy, Dan M., 32, 787
Lambert, Richard D., 166, 313, 487-89
Langlois, Walter G., 167
Lasker, Gabriel W., 114
Laves, Walter H. C., 20, 60, 686, 704, 739
Lawson, Edwin D., 740
Leavitt, Howard B., 788
Leavy, Sylvia S., 451
Lee, Muna, 289
Legters, Lyman H., 94-95, 110-11, 874
Leonard, Elizabeth W., 352
Lesser, Simon O., 567
Leuallen, Dean E. Emerson, 411
Lewis, Martin Deming, 112
Lippitt, Ronald, 313, 412, 490-91, 533
Little, J. Kenneth, 725
Liu, James T. C., 168
Long, Lewis M. K., 492
Loomis, Charles P., 493
Lorenz, Reuben, 413
Lorge, Irving, 543

Lowry, W. McNeil, 658
Lundstedt, Sven, 494
Lysgaard, Sverre, 495

McCabe, Sumie F., 272
McClelland, Charles A., 61
McClintock, Charles G., 496
McConnell, John W., 731
MacCormac, Kenneth, 625
McCullough, Mabelle G., 414
McGee, Gale W., 82
McGovern, George, 689
McGrath, Earl J., 21
Macgregor, Gordon, 271, 362
McGuigan, F. J., 353
McKeon, Richard, 22
McKnight, Robert K., 461-64
McMurry, Ruth E., 289
McNamara, Robert S., 678-79, 687
McNiff, Phillip J., 113
Maddox, James G., 568
Madow, Pauline, 251
Malik, Charles H., 23, 272, 626
Mandelbaum, David Goodman 114
Mandell, Milton M., 223
Mangone, Gerard J., 208-10, 224, 237
Manning, Clarence A., 195
Marckwardt, Albert H., 95
Maretzki, T., 252
Marin, Juan, 741
Marquardt, William F., 497
Marriott, McKim, 114, 169
Marron, James M., 115
Marsh, Gayle G., 498
Marvel, William W., 24-5, 789
Masland, John Wesley, 225

AUTHOR INDEX

Matthew, R. J., 335
Melady, Thomas P., 116
Melby, John F., 272, 499
Mendelsohn, Harold, 363
Mestenhauser, Josef A., 307, 414, 675
Metraux, Guy S., 290, 313
Meyer, Samuel L., 184
Michigan State University, 141
Mildenberger, Kenneth W., 95
Miller, Walter W., 581
Mills, Richard C., 500
Milstein, Elliott, 501
Minor, Harold B., 272
Mischel, Walter, 502
Mogannam, E. Theodore, 641
Montgomery, John D., 226
Mooney, Francis E., Jr., 790
Moore, Forrest G., 272, 627
Morehouse, Ward, 62, 95, 117-20, 170-72, 196
Morgan, Gordon D., 416
Morgan, Theodore, 227
Morgenthau, Hans J., 63
Morot-Sir, Edouard, 272
Morrill, J. L., 38
Morris, Richard T., 487, 503, 525
Morse, Richard M., 95
Morton, Louis, 121
Mosely, Philip E., 197
Moses, Larry, 838
Mosher, Arthur Theodore, 791
Mosher, Frederick C., 792
Mulligan, Agnes C., 553
Murase, Kenneth, 418
Murphy, E. J., 419
Murphy, Franklin D., 64
Myers, Charles A., 778-79
Myers, Charles Nash, 793

Nakaya, Kenichi, 291
Nason, John W., 26, 54
National Academy of Sciences--National Research Council, 768
National Association for Foreign Student Affairs, 309, 377-78 556, 839
National Association of State Universities and Land-Grant Colleges, 410
National Catholic Educational Association, 830
National Citizens' Commission on International Cooperation, 31
National Council of Applied Economic Research, New Delhi, 628
National Institute of Psychology, Tehran, 607
National Planning Association, 802
Neal, Joe W., 27, 272, 420
Nehnevjsa, J., 504
Nelson, Charles A., 11
Nelson, Robert L., 421-22
Neumeyer, Martin H., 423
New York State Education Department, 74, 79, 84
Newman, Sidney H., 221
Niebuhr, Reinhold, 65
Niehoff, Arthur H., 200
Nielsen, Marion L., 104
Nielsen, Waldemar A., 505
Niyekawa, Agnes M., 629

O'Grady, Lorraine, 691
Olsen, Erling, 424
Olsen, Lionel R., 507
Orenstein, Frank E., 363
Otis, Jack, 426

Pabsch, Weigand, 675
Pace, Charles R., 336
Palmer, Archie M., 124
Parker, Franklin, 675, 742
Parker, William Riley, 66-67
Parsons, Kenneth H., 427

Parthemos, George S., 28
Pasamanick, Benjamin, 510-11
Passin, Herbert, 463-64, 487
Peace Corps, 690
Pedram, Manouchehr, 508
Peter, Hollis W., 229, 567, 632
Peterson, James A., 423
Pett, Dennis W., 796
Phillips, Claude S., Jr., 29
Phillips, Ethel C., 30
Pierson, Constance L., 691
Platt, Joseph B., 428
Porter, Robert D., 308, 442
Porter, Willis P., 667
Poujol, Jacques, 675
Pratt, Dallas, 264, 429
Preston, Harley O., 233
Prewitt, Charles W., 799
Princeton University, 128, 133
Pritchard, Edith M., 430
Public Administration Clearing House, 230, 232
Putnam, Ivan, Jr., 272, 877

Quattlebaum, Charles A., 693

Radway, Laurence I., 225
Randall, Helen W., 337
Rathore, Naeem G., 509
Raushenbush, Esther, 431
Rawson, Harve E., 512
Redefer, Frederick L., 68
Reed, Howard A., 125-26
Reining, Conrad C., 95, 140
Reining, Henry, Jr., 800
Rettig, Salomon, 510-13
Revelle, Roger, 658
Rhoades, Margaret M., 843

Riegel, Oscar W., 514
Robbins, John, 173
Roberts, Henry L., 95
Robinson, Mary E., 801
Rose, Alvin W., 803
Rose, Arnold M., 515
Rosenzweig, Robert M., 695, 729
Roskens, Ronald W., 544
Rostow, W. W., 783
Roth, Sidney G., 444
Roucek, Joseph S., 667
Rowen, Henry S., 730
Ruedisili, Chester H., 432
Ruffner, Ralph W., 805-6
Rupard, Robert, 13
Rusk, Dean, 13

Sabrosky, Laurel K., 633-34
Saccio, Leonard J., 13
Samper, Armando, 807
Sanders, Irwin T., 231, 433
Sasnett, Martena T., 516, 557-58
Sathyamurthy, T. V., 743-44
Sayre, Joan M., 434
Sayre, Wallace S., 232
Sayres, William C., 130
Scanlon, David G., 33
Schild, Erling O., 303, 350-51, 467
Schlesinger, Ben, 569
Schlesinger, Lawrence E., 632
Schmidt, J. P., 435
Schmidt, Liselotte, 880
Schuler, Edgar A., 493
Schwantes, Robert S., 291-92
Scigliano, Robert G., 808
Scott, Franklin D., 313, 487, 517, 635
Selby, Henry A., 518
Selltiz, Claire, 467, 469, 519-21, 525
Sewell, William H., 487, 522, 525

AUTHOR INDEX

Shaffer, Robert H., 523
Shaftel, F. R., 253
Shank, Donald J., 32, 272, 338-40, 436, 442
Sharp, Paul F., 275
Shimbori, Michiya, 276
Shinagel, Michael, 254
Shively, Stanley E., 478 524
Shiver, Elizabeth N., 731
Shuster, George N., 658, 745
Silvert, Kalman H., 732
Sinauer, Ernst M., 699
Singer, Milton B., 95, 131, 174
Singh, Paras N., 513
Sinor, Denis, 95
Sloan, Ruth C., 437
Smith, Bradford, 636
Smith, Bruce L., 809
Smith, Howard P., 637-38
Smith, J. Paul, 264
Smith, M. Brewster, 255-56, 264, 310-12, 494, 525-26, 639
Smuckler, Ralph H., 810-11
Smythe, H. and M. M., 438
Southern Association of Colleges and Schools, 15
Speakman, Cummins E., Jr., 277
Spector, Paul, 233
Spence, Ralph B., 640, 812
Spencer, Richard E., 527
Springer, George P., 272
Stabler, John B., 641
Stalker, John N., 234
Stamm, Ester F., 83
Stearns, Troy L., 439
Stevenson, Adlai E., 675
Stevenson, William E., 34
Stieglitz, Francine B., 541
Stone, Donald C., 257, 278
Storey, Robert G., 279

Storm, William B., 440, 813
Strain, William H., 441-42, 559-62
Suchman, Edward A., 525
Swanson, Gordon I., 667
Swift, Richard N., 69
Syracuse University, 319

Taba, Hilda, 313, 342
Taggart, Glen L., 35
Tandler, Fredrika M., 868
Tanenhaus, Joseph, 444, 528
Taper, B., 814
Taylor, George E., 95, 192, 730
Taylor, Harold, 36, 667
Tead, Ordway, 70
Technical Assistance Clearing House, 852
Teichert, Pedro C. M., 132
Teng, S. Y., 175
Tewksbury, Donald G., 37
Thomas, R. Murray, 815
Thompson, John M., 191, 193
Thompson, Ronald Burdick, 564
Thomson, Charles A., 704, 739
Thurber, Clarence E., 232, 570-71
Thurston, John L., 445
Tierney, Hannelore, 115
Tolley, Howard R., 568
Torre, Mottram, 235
Trent, W. J., Jr., 446
Tryon, Ruth W., 296
Tyler, Ralph W., 545
Tyrrell, William G., 71

United Nations Educational, Scientific and Cultural Organization, 142, 846, 849-50, 853
United Nations Secretariat, 770

United States Advisory Commission on International Educational and Cultural Affairs, 269, 656, 698
United States Agency for International Development, 572, 609-10, 631, 643, 652, 661, 705-6, 710, 715, 784
United States Bureau of Educational and Cultural Affairs, 611, 665, 673, 837, 845, 851, 870-71
United States Bureau of European Affairs, 701
United States Bureau of Intelligence and Research, 700, 730, 838, 843, 865
United States Bureau of the Budget, 727
United States Congress, House of Representatives, Committee on Foreign Affairs, 654, 657, 678, 713, 856
United States Congress, Senate, Committee on Foreign Relations, 199, 236, 679, 733
United States Department of Agriculture, 655
United States Department of Defense, 707-8
United States Department of State, 280, 529, 608, 668, 672, 711, 827
United States Educational Commission in Japan, 295
United States Educational Commission in the United Kingdom, 293
United States High Commissioner for Germany, 644-45
United States Information Service, Taiwan, 630
United States International Educational Exchange Service, 288
United States National Commission for UNESCO, 84
United States National Student Association, 369, 857
United States Office of Education, 80, 684, 703, 840, 858
United States Operations Mission to Indonesia, 646
United States Operations Mission to Vietnam, 563
University of California, 181, 825
University of Hawaii, 448-49
University of Helsinki, 614
University of Michigan, 506, 598
University of Wisconsin, 824
Useem, John and Ruth H., 281, 313, 487, 647

Van Mook, H. J., 574
Van Neil, Robert, 176
Vent, Myron H., 816
Veroff, Joseph, 494
Viederman, Stephen, 282

Wallace, John A., 344
Waltman, Howard L., 575
Walton, Barbara J., 451
Walton, D. Michael, 531-32
Wang, Joan Parsons, 821
Wann, Kenneth D., 214
Ward, Douglas S., 452
Ward, F. Champion, 134
Warmbrunn, Werner, 313, 648
Watanabe, J., 264
Watson, Curtis B., 345

AUTHOR INDEX

Watson, Jeanne, 313, 412, 490-91, 533
Weaver, Paul, 346
Weidner, Edward W., 39, 347, 571
Weidner, Jean B., 347
Weiner, Myron, 177
Wells, Herman B, 712, 734
Welty, Paul S., 85
Wengert, Egbert S., 237
Wharton, Clifton R., Jr., 576
Wheatley, Charles W., 534
Whitaker, Urban, 135
White, Aurilla, 854-55
Whyte, William Foote, 220
Wilder, Emilia, 535
Williams, David B., 453
Williams, E. I. F., 454
Williams, Herbert H., 455-56
Williams, Robin M., Jr., 525
Willner, A. R., 238
Wilson, Charles R., 72
Wilson, Elmo C., 589

Wilson, Florence H., 42
Wilson, Howard E., 32, 40-42, 86, 658
Wingenbach, Charles E., 258
Witt, Lawrence, 817
Wolf, Charles, Jr., 730
Wolf, Elinor K., 272, 499
Won, George Y. M., 494
Woodrow Wilson School of Public and International Affairs, 651
Woods, Clyde M., 518
Woodyatt, Philip C., 458
World Affairs Center, 829
World Health Organization, 450
Wright, Arthur F., 178
Wyatt, Donald W., 505

Yalem, Ronald J., 73
Young, Francis A., 283-84, 714

Zajonc, Robert B., 536

ABOUT THE AUTHORS

Richard F. Crabbs is Dean of the Faculties at The American University in Cairo, Cairo, Egypt. He has also served as Executive Secretary of the Committee on International Affairs, Indiana University, and as Assistant to the Executive Secretary, U.S. Educational Foundation in India. He has taught international relations at the University of Denver and Indiana University. Dr. Crabbs received his Ph.D. degree from Stanford University.

Frank W. Holmquist is a Ph.D. candidate in government at Indiana University and has received an NDEA-related Fulbright-Hays Award for Advanced Research in Kenya.

Z
5814
U7C7   APR 25 1968